What Readers .
Good Boundaries and Goodbyes

"This is the book I wish someone had given me at the start of my journey as a Jesus follower. I was so emotionally wounded from traumatic experiences in my past that I didn't know how to set healthy boundaries, nor when to say necessary goodbyes. As a result, I experienced relational fractures that caused much pain and could have been avoided by applying the hard-earned wisdom shared within these pages. In *Good Boundaries and Goodbyes*, Lysa unpacks important principles and dispels destructive fallacies that will help you to honor God and flourish in life by setting healthy boundaries and embracing necessary goodbyes."

—Christine Caine, founder of A21 and Propel Women

"In a world that talks a lot *about* boundaries, Lysa gently guides us to understand *why* they are critical to the loving relationships we crave and shows us how to do them well. By reframing boundaries from something that can feel *limiting* to something that is truly *loving*, this book equips us to navigate relationships in a loving, healthy, and God-honoring way. If you ever feel as though you're stuck between being taken advantage of by those you love most or shutting others out to avoid being hurt, *Good Boundaries and Goodbyes* will provide both the practical and biblical guidance you need to operate in the most loving place, with healthy boundaries instead of either extreme."

—Jordan Lee Dooley, *Wall Street Journal* bestselling author

"Once again, Lysa does what she does best by gently guiding us through something hard that all of us will have to make decisions about—boundaries in our relationships. If you are like me, these conversations about boundaries make me nervous and fearful. In *Good Boundaries and Goodbyes*, Lysa uses her own journey as an encouragement to us all. I finished the last page of this book and cried. Tears of encouragement and hope for those relationships that I know will be healthier after having some hard conversations about boundaries. Thank you, Lysa, for helping us! Everyone needs this book!"

—Jamie Ivey, bestselling author and host of
The Happy Hour with Jamie Ivey podcast

"Written in the tone of a wise, loving girlfriend who has your best interest at heart, this book had me highlighting something on just about every page! . . . I kept reading parts of it out loud to myself because I found it so profound."

—Shanae G.

"What a gift this book is! Lysa's words have been soaked in countless hours of study in God's Word and weighed with grace and mercy in real-life experiences. This book has changed every false belief I entertained about boundaries for the good!"

—Melanie P.

"Lysa does an amazing job of sharing her raw, vulnerable, and heartfelt experiences, lessons, and hurts. Reading her words has made me feel seen and understood in a way not many authors can. I am so grateful that she has been willing to share her life, pains, and joys with the rest of us. I can't wait to give this book to my close friends, hoping it will help them as much as it's helped me."

—Amy H.

"Lysa's words and faith-based perspective in this book helped me cultivate boundaries in my own life that I didn't realize I needed. This encouragement has been a blessing and equipped me to strengthen some of my closest relationships."

—Hope H.

"This book is for the girl with a wide-open heart who needs some guidance about when to say no, how to set boundaries without guilt, and what words to speak in those hard moments. Lysa always reminds me to keep my heart safe and how to truly honor our God."

—Sanaz W.

GOOD
BOUNDARIES
AND
GOODBYES

Other Books and Video Bible Studies by Lysa

Children's

GOOD

BOUNDARIES

AND

GOODBYES

LOVING OTHERS WITHOUT LOSING
THE BEST OF WHO YOU ARE

LYSA TERKEURST

NELSON
BOOKS

An Imprint of Thomas Nelson

Published in Nashville, Tennessee, by Nelson Books, an imprint of Thomas Nelson. Nelson Books and Thomas Nelson are registered trademarks of HarperCollins Christian Publishing, Inc.

Thomas Nelson titles may be purchased in bulk for educational, business, fundraising, or sales promotional use. For information, please e-mail SpecialMarkets@ThomasNelson.com.

Unless otherwise noted, Scripture quotations taken from The Holy Bible, New International Version®, NIV®. Copyright © 1973, 1978, 1984, 2011 by Biblica, Inc.® Used by permission of Zondervan. All rights reserved worldwide. www.Zondervan.com. The "NIV" and "New International Version" are trademarks registered in the United States Patent and Trademark Office by Biblica, Inc.®

Scripture quotations marked THE MESSAGE are taken from *THE MESSAGE.* Copyright © 1993, 2002, 2018 by Eugene H. Peterson. Used by permission of NavPress. All rights reserved. Represented by Tyndale House Publishers, Inc.

Scripture quotations marked ESV are taken from the ESV® Bible (The Holy Bible, English Standard Version®). Copyright © 2001 by Crossway, a publishing ministry of Good News Publishers. Used by permission. All rights reserved.

Scripture quotations marked NKJV are taken from the New King James Version®. Copyright © 1982 by Thomas Nelson. Used by permission. All rights reserved.

Any internet addresses, phone numbers, or company or product information printed in this book are offered as a resource and are not intended in any way to be or to imply an endorsement by Thomas Nelson, nor does Thomas Nelson vouch for the existence, content, or services of these sites, phone numbers, companies, or products beyond the life of this book.

Library of Congress Cataloging-in-Publication Data

Names: TerKeurst, Lysa, author.
Title: Good boundaries and goodbyes : loving others without losing the best of who you are / Lysa TerKeurst.
Description: Nashville : Thomas Nelson, [2022] | Summary: "Number-one New York Times bestselling author Lysa TerKeurst helps readers stop the dysfunction of unhealthy relationships by showing them biblical ways to set boundaries--and, when necessary, say goodbye--without losing the best of who they are"-- Provided by publisher.
Identifiers: LCCN 2022017973 (print) | LCCN 2022017974 (ebook) | ISBN 9781400211760 (hardcover) | ISBN 9781400211791 (ebook) | ISBN 9781400211807 (audiobook) | ISBN 9781400239863 (IE)
Subjects: LCSH: Interpersonal relations--Religious aspects--Christianity. | Love--Religious aspects--Christianity.
Classification: LCC BV4597.52 .T39 2022 (print) | LCC BV4597.52 (ebook) | DDC 241/.4--dc23/eng/20220728
LC record available at https://lccn.loc.gov/2022017973
LC ebook record available at https://lccn.loc.gov/2022017974

Printed in the United States of America

22 23 24 25 26 LSC 10 9 8 7 6 5 4 3 2 1

I dedicate this message to the courageous woman who will make some hard but very brave decisions to step out of chaos toward health and honesty. I thought about you as I wrote every word of this book. Remember when you love deeply you may get hurt deeply. But getting hurt doesn't mean you have to fear closeness with all people. It actually means you have a tremendous capacity to love others really well because you dared to offer another person the most tender depths of your heart. Don't pack love away like an old sweater you never want to wear again. Good boundaries can help you recognize what got unraveled so you can love others without losing the best of who you are. Tucked within these pages, are thousands of my tears that dripped into smudges of ink as I promised God that if He would help me live this message, I would write this message. And that I would do everything possible to get this book into your hands. It's such an honor to meet you here. Now, let's get started together.

♡

Contents

Introduction

We Can't Set Good Boundaries Without Love

Well, hello. There's so much I want to write in these first words to provide the right environment for this book. I wish I could hand you your favorite coffee, toss you a blanket, set a box of tissues on the table in front of us, put on just the right soundtrack, and catch up on where we both are in life.

I would so much rather talk all of this through face-to-face. Or at least write this to you in a letter in my own handwriting. There's a deeply human element that I don't want to get lost in these black-and-white pages and words typed with a computer font. We're both picking up this book in the middle of real life where we're navigating what works and what doesn't in the relationships we treasure.

And because relationships are so very organic, they move like breath in and out of our lungs, expanding with deep connection one minute and in the next atrophying into complete misunderstanding. Relationships are wonderful and full of love and frustration and wrought with angst and all the things we bring into every attempted embrace with another person. When those we love draw close to us, they draw close to our issues. And we come face-to-face with their issues as well.

And as we open up to each other, the deeper we connect, the more vulnerable we become. The more vulnerable we become, the more exposed the tender places inside of us become. This exposure is risky. When we dare to be so very known, we risk being so very hurt. When we dare to be so very hopeful, we risk being so very disappointed. When we dare to be so very giving, we risk being so very taken advantage of. And when we dare to unnaturally change into what someone else needs, we risk losing ourselves in the process.

To love and be loved is to be enveloped in the safest feeling I've ever known.

To cause hurt and be hurt is to be crushed with the scariest feeling I've ever known.

You and I both know this. In different ways with different people and to varying degrees, we know the multifaceted complications of love and heartbreak.

We dream of the best, we dread the worst, and we keep trying to figure out how to do relationships right. We build our lives around those we love. And those we love build their lives around us.

We laugh and connect and disconnect and fight and make up and coast and drift and come back and think about how lucky we are to be with someone until we send our counselor the broken heart emoji with the text, "Need help now . . . this isn't going well." Or maybe we use other words and emojis we can't really put right here in this little book.

It's just not all magical like the plots of the Hallmark Christmas movies.

People in these movies seem to live with the blessing of predictability and things always epically working out. There's never a need for ongoing boundaries because there are no ongoing hardships. Once the story turns for good, it stays good until the credits roll.

Last week I sent a text to my friends after watching too many of these movies. It was my attempt at correcting these unrealistic plots. And it went like this:

> **OPENING SCENE:** Snow falling gently on townspeople smiling, laughing, ice skating. Girl is serving customers in the midst of everyone else's fun. She has an unreasonable, mean boss. She looks out of sorts, like she's searching for something, something that's just beyond her grasp. Suddenly a man with a guitar, smug attitude, and unusual fame appears. And he's a secret prince from a far-off land. She spills water on him. He writes her a song. They fall in love.
> **CLOSING SCENE:** She becomes a princess.

But unfortunately, we all know that's unrealistic. Life doesn't tie up in a neat, nice bow. So, really the script should go like this:

> **OPENING SCENE:** Same beginning scenario, but . . . she spills water on the guy, he freaks out, doesn't leave a tip, tries to get her fired, and she goes home mumbling about what a jerk he was. Also, his castle is in foreclosure and soon he's working as a busboy at the same restaurant. She's eventually promoted to manager, becomes independently successful, and she sets boundaries with him because he's being irresponsible in the way he closes out the registers each night. Then she makes some discoveries that cause her to fire him because he's stealing from the cash drawer.
> **CLOSING SCENE:** She buys the castle and invites her friends over to process what went wrong with him and how in the world he could steal from her! But then, after the closing scene, she questions herself over and over and still wishes things could have been different.

Obviously, Hallmark isn't clamoring for me to write for them anytime soon.

But I am eager to process what I believe has been the missing piece in the storyline of my relationships for far too long: *good boundaries*.

Now, this is where I want to look straight into your eyes and say something really important. This isn't a book about leaving people. It's a book about loving people in right and healthy ways. And it's about communicating appropriate boundaries and parameters so that love can stay safe and sustainable. Boundaries aren't meant to shove love away. Quite the opposite. We set boundaries so we know what to do when we very much want to love those around us really well without losing ourselves in the process. Good boundaries help us preserve the love within us even when some relationships become unsustainable and we must accept the reality of a goodbye.

Throughout these pages we'll seek to honestly examine what is and is not healthy in our hearts but also in the relationships where we invest our hearts. Sometimes it's difficult to know what's healthy and what's not, so it's important to seek godly counsel and, in more complex situations like addictions and abuse, someone specifically trained on the issues at hand. (Please see "Getting the Help You Need" on page 231.)

After all, God's ultimate assignment is for us to love Him and love others. And this is exactly what Jesus taught and modeled. "A new command I give you: Love one another. As I have loved you, so you must love one another" (John 13:34).

But we can't enable bad behavior in ourselves and others and call it love. We can't tolerate destructive patterns and call it love. And we can't pride ourselves on being loyal and longsuffering in our relationships when it's really perpetuating violations of what

We can't enable bad behavior and call it love.

God says love is. Please hear me clearly say, the purpose of this book isn't to quickly call out issues in others without looking honestly at ourselves as well. We need to examine our motivations and our mindsets.

And this isn't a message that is encouraging people to divorce quickly, thoughtlessly, or unadvisedly. Proverbs 15:22 reminds us that there is wisdom in a multitude of counselors. This also isn't a message about encouraging people to abandon others just because things get difficult or the other person is walking through a hard season.

But we also don't need to swing the pendulum to the extreme where we stay in a destructive, toxic, or abusive relationship no matter what. (See "Some Important Notes to Consider on Abuse" page 232.) Boundaries, as you will soon see, should help us avoid extremes and live closer to the kind of love God intended for relationships.

Love must be honest. Love must be safe. Love must seek each person's highest good.

And love must honor God to experience the fullness and the freedom of the sweetest connection between two humans.

In fact, when I turn to 1 Corinthians 13:4–7, I'm reminded of God's intention for the purest form of love. Here's how I journaled what I want to remember from these scriptures:

Love is not dishonorable.
Love does not justify wrongs to enable selfishness.

Love does not celebrate evil.

Love requires truth.

Love leads to honor, kindness, and compassion.

So, as we take this journey, let's remember the real purpose of good boundaries. Boundaries protect the right kind of love and help prevent dysfunction from destroying that love. Boundaries help us say what needs to be said, do what needs to be done, and establish what is and isn't acceptable. Love should be what draws us together not what tears us apart.

And, remember, we can't set good boundaries without love. Setting boundaries from a place of anger and bitterness will only lead to control and manipulation. Setting boundaries as a punishment will only serve to imprison us. But setting boundaries from a place of love provides an opportunity for relationships to grow deeply because true connection thrives within the safety of health and honesty.

I guess my greatest fear in writing this book after an unwanted divorce is that it might seem I'm eager to push others away. But that's not true. I'm more eager than ever before to deeply love the people in my life. And I know how destructive it can be to navigate relationship devastation because of a lack of boundaries. I know what it feels like to be paralyzed by another person's choices that break your heart over and over and not know what to do about it. I know the frustration of saying something has to change but feeling stuck when the other person isn't cooperating with those needed changes. So while some relationships become unsustainable to the point that it's necessary to move beyond a good boundary to a goodbye, you don't have to become someone you were never meant to be.

When we're hurt, good boundaries and goodbyes help us to not get stuck in a perpetual state of living hurt.

Love should be what

draws us together not

what tears us apart.

— Ups

> When we're hurt, good
> boundaries and goodbyes
> help us to not get stuck in a
> perpetual state of living hurt.

This is a book written to help you discover that good boundaries can pave the road for the truest and purest version of love to emerge within the relationships that make up so much of who we are and what we want the most.

As we process good boundaries and learn more about goodbyes throughout the book, I've created a section at the end of each chapter called, "Now, Let's Live This." It's a wrap-up of what we're reading and learning and includes some questions and scriptures to ponder as we go. Remember, this isn't just a message to read, it's one we will want to sit with, wrestle through, and process in prayer. Then, if we want real transformation, we'll have to take the crucial step of application.

This won't be the easiest message to apply to your life, but it will likely be one of the most valuable steps you take toward emotional health and better relationships. And the best part of it all, you won't be alone. I'll be with you as we trust God to lead us through every word and every next step. And you'll also hear from my Christian counselor Jim Cress, who will weigh in with therapeutic insights throughout the book.

Now, Let's Live This . . .

REMEMBER (STATEMENTS TO CLING TO):

- We can't enable bad behavior and call it love.
- Love must honor God to experience the fullness and the freedom of the sweetest connection between two humans.
- Boundaries protect the right kind of love and help prevent dysfunction from destroying that love.
- Love should be what draws us together not what tears us apart.
- Setting boundaries from a place of love provides an opportunity for relationships to grow deeply because true connection thrives within the safety of health and honesty.
- When we're hurt, good boundaries and goodbyes help us to not get stuck in a perpetual state of living hurt.

RECEIVE (SCRIPTURES TO SOAK IN):

"A new command I give you: Love one another. As I have loved you, so you must love one another." (John 13:34)

Love is patient, love is kind. It does not envy, it does not boast, it is not proud. It does not dishonor others, it is not self-seeking, it is not easily angered, it keeps no record of wrongs. Love does not delight in evil but rejoices with the truth. It always protects, always trusts, always hopes, always perseveres. (1 Corinthians 13:4–7)

REFLECT (QUESTIONS TO THINK THROUGH):

- Have you ever considered that establishing healthy parameters in your relationships is actually an act of love? As you start this book, how does this change your perspective?

- What may have motivated you in the past to set boundaries or say a goodbye? Take time to think this through and then write down your answers.
- When you're in a relationship where there's been chaos, confusion, and hurt, reacting in extremes can add even more pain. Some people take on all the blame and minimize the actions of the other person. The opposite extreme is to place sole blame on the other person without checking your own heart. Throughout this book, we want to avoid going to either of these extremes. So, honest self-reflection is always a good practice. Asking yourself these questions is a wise step now, and revisiting them before you set a boundary or say goodbye could also be helpful:
  — Have I set unrealistic expectations?
  — Am I too easily offended?
  — Have I considered my own shortcomings relative to this relationship?
  — Have I sought wisdom from a godly advisor, mentor, or counselor?

PRAYER:

Lord, the greatest desire of my heart is to love and treasure others the way You treasure us. But honestly, sometimes these hard relationship dynamics make it incredibly difficult to discern what is truly loving. So, as I turn these next pages, I ask that You guide me and help me to walk in Your ways, not mine. Show me how to approach my closest relationships with both compassion and a healthy commitment to reality so I am in alignment with You. In Jesus' name, amen.

CHAPTER 1

You Are Not Crazy
(You can love them, but
you can't change them.)

"You cannot build trust that keeps getting broken." Those words were coming to me in impossible waves of grief, bumping into the still-raw places of my heart. I waffled from wanting to scream those words to wanting to take them back and swallow them whole.

Before this moment, I'd only been able to write them in my journal. But then, in an unplanned moment of stinging honesty, I spoke them out loud. First to my counselor, then, later, to the man I had been married to for nearly three decades.

"You cannot build trust that keeps getting broken." It was a gut punch. It can be awful to speak the truth sometimes. And yet, it is much more awful to have truth staring you in the face and deny it.

I loved him. I treasured our long talks processing life and love and even all the everyday stuff that builds close connection. Back when things were normal, I assumed this relationship would always be a big part of my life. But then things started to change, deteriorate, and flip everything upside down. Lies became more common than truth. Second chances turned into third and fourth and fiftieth chances to right the wrongs with truth.

Promises were made.

And, for a season, promises were kept. But just when I thought we were getting somewhere, promises were broken.

The problem is that trust is an incredibly fragile thing to rebuild. The setbacks are cruel. Unexpected sprains are debilitating. And if twisted backward to the point of fracture, the splinters of trust broken over and over are daggers to the heart.

Every bit of me wanted our marriage to be healthy and thriving. And yet everything about reality demanded that changes be made.

The addictions were back. And so were the violations of clearly established boundaries. I could not ignore it or pretend to be okay with it. Every time I saw new evidence, I recoiled both from the pain inside my chest and the piercing flashbacks in my brain. My counselor calls these "triggers." Each time I was triggered, I was transported back to the time when I didn't understand addictions. I didn't understand that good people can do really bad things when addictions take over. I thought I was going crazy.

Seeing evidence of the addictions again screamed terrorizing warnings: "You aren't safe. It's happening again. Everything is a lie. You're about to get blindsided. You won't survive this."

I shook my head. My body folded in half. And sobs erupted from the depths of my being. I had given every bit of love and forgiveness I knew to give, and it wasn't enough. Love given is wildly beautiful. Love received is wildly fulfilling. But for love to thrive as true and lasting, it must be within the safety of trust. Without trust, love will die. So, I had to say it: "You cannot build trust that keeps getting broken."

And as I let the words out, I felt as if I was declaring one of the worst defeats of my life. I had the wrong notion that to be a Christian requires that we believe the best no matter what. That it's unkind to draw boundaries. That it's noble and commendable to stay in a relationship no matter what. I no longer believe that.

I now believe we must honor what honors God. And in doing so, we must not confuse the good commands to love and forgive with the bad realities of enabling and covering up things that are not honoring to God. When someone's dishonorable actions beg us not to stay, this should give us serious pause.

My counselor, Jim Cress, once held up a pillow in between my face and his own. He said, "When you are speaking to this person, everything you say must pass through the addictions first. You aren't talking to the person you love."

I knew Jim was right. I kept trying to have a conversation with the irrationality of substances that could only allow me to be either the enabler or the enemy. The enabler will be manipulated. The enemy will be lied to. Either way, there is no love in manipulations and lies. Love breathes the oxygen of trust. Love struggles and eventually becomes strangled in the oxygen-depleted grapple of addictions.

Though I wasn't the one choosing the addictive substances, I was the one now drawing a line that could not be crossed another time. But deep down, I knew the boundary would be crossed just as it had many times before.

The seduction of his many addictions had so captured him that I now knew I wasn't really talking to the man I loved.

His eyes were the same shape I'd looked in countless times, but his truest self wasn't there. He could not see what I was seeing. He

We must not confuse the good

commands to love and forgive

with the bad realities of enabling

and covering up things that

are not honoring to God.

— Lys

would not hear what I was saying. Though we were only a few feet apart, there was a chasm between us.

Health cannot bond with unhealth.

So, either I had to get unhealthy and enable this cycle to continue, or I had to follow through with the boundaries we had agreed upon. In a time of renewal, we had written out what would and would not be acceptable in our relationship moving forward. And now, the realities of those broken vows were a crushing blow.

I hadn't wanted to admit that the addictions were surfacing and spiraling again. To admit that would force me to make the choice to once again turn this man I loved over to his choices. To stop the madness, I would have to let go of his hand. Let go of what had been such a big part of my life. Stop myself from stepping in to rescue him over and over. And then remind myself to breathe a thousand painful and fearful breaths every single day. I knew at some point I would stare at my face in the mirror and wonder, *But what if I rescued him this time and it finally turned everything around? Or what if I don't rescue him and something terrible happens? Will I regret this for the rest of my life? Is there anything else I can do?*

Yet because of all the wise counsel I'd gotten, there was nothing else to do. And it felt like a shameful defeat to me. It's hard to own what you don't choose. I knew I shouldn't own the repercussions of addictions that weren't mine. But when your life is so tightly woven into a collective fabric of a close relationship, it can be excruciatingly maddening to watch someone choose things you know are destructive. Though their choices are their own, the consequences have an impact on everyone who loves them, much like exploding hand grenades. You don't have to be the one to pull the pin to be deeply devastated by the resulting shrapnel.

You can't reason with a person caught in the addiction cycle any more than you can try to talk a live grenade out of exploding.

When the pin is pulled a chain of events is set off that creates destruction. Most people struggling with addictions will have irrational justifications that will never make sense. They don't factor in others. They truly think their choices only affect them.

They don't feel your heartbreak.

They don't want to see your tears.

They will tell you that the blue sky is orange . . . that the orange car is green . . . that their glass is full of one thing when you absolutely know it's something else. And when their lies hit you without even a twitch of remorse from them, you wonder if any truth exists between you at all.

If you go with what they say, you'll become more and more convinced you're the problem. If you oppose what they say, they will make sure you feel you are definitely the problem.

Either way, you lose.

And I was losing . . . my health, my emotional well-being and, even if I didn't want to admit it, my marriage.

So, now the only real choice I had to make was whether or not to lose with my sanity intact.

I realize that more severe issues like addiction may not be what's making some of your relationships incredibly challenging. There are so many reasons relationships can start to slip from being healthy to unhealthy. Or, at least from fulfilling to frustrating.

Relationships are wonderful until they're not. But most of us aren't nearly as equipped as we need to be to know what to do when we know things need to change but the other person isn't willing to or capable of cooperating with the needed changes.

Or your challenge may be with a great person, and you can't figure out how to address something that is bothering you or how to communicate the need for a boundary.

Or it may be with a person in authority over you and boundaries don't feel like they would work.

Or it's with a family member who lives in your home, and though you need some distance, setting a boundary doesn't feel very realistic.

All relationships can be difficult at times, but they should not be destructive to our well-being. If you have relationships in your life where you know something is wrong, but you can't for the life of you figure out what to do, I believe you'll quickly find the reason you need this book. I understand what it feels like to have your body tense and your pulse quicken while your mind is screaming at the other person, "Stop doing this!" You've prayed about this behavior or situation. You've talked about this. You've tried to navigate it. You may have even tried to stop it. But in the end, nothing has worked.

You've reached a place where you know you can forgive the person. And you can love them. You want to save the relationship and get to a better place more than anything. You've made changes. You've listened to wise advice and done everything you know to do. But you've finally realized if they don't want things to change, you cannot change them. And now you're secretly starting to wonder if you are the crazy one.

Friend, you may be brokenhearted. You may be sad. You may be afraid and possibly angry. You may be focused on trying to fix what isn't within your ability to fix. And you may even be fixated on trying to figure everything out.

But you are not crazy. If you are smelling smoke, there is fire. And the only reasonable option at this point is to either put out the fire or get yourself out of the fire.

Drawing boundaries can help put out fires before they become all consuming. But if the fire keeps burning with increasing intensity, you've got to get away from the smoke and flames. Sometimes, your only option is to say goodbye.

I hope you'll soon see that boundaries aren't just a good idea, they are a God idea. Boundaries are woven into everything God has done since the very beginning. We'll get to that in the coming chapters. But think about this for now: God even put an actual boundary around the sea during creation. The sea would eventually be known to the people who lived during biblical times as a symbol of chaos. So, the boundary for the sea was a barrier of sand placed by God that the chaos was not allowed to cross (Jeremiah 5:22).

Where there is an abundance of chaos, there is usually a lack of good boundaries. Chaos shouldn't be the norm and while we can't always change the source of the chaos, we must tend to what we can change. Please know: it's not unchristian to set these healthy parameters. It's not unchristian to require people to treat you in healthy ways. And for us to do the same for others. It's not unchristian to call wrong things wrong and hurtful things hurtful. We can do it all with honor, kindness, and love, but we have to know how to spot dysfunction, what to do about it, and when to recognize it's no longer reasonable or safe to stay in some relationships.

Like the other books I've written, this is a message I need most of all. I'm still challenged by setting and keeping boundaries. I've come to understand that boundaries aren't a method to perfect but rather an opportunity to protect what God intended for relationships.

I need that and I imagine you might too.

And we'll also look at goodbyes. We all have relationships that didn't last like we thought they would. But most of us find these endings incredibly confusing and sometimes crushing. Maybe you've wondered like me if it's even possible for a goodbye to be good at all?

If you have questions and hesitations about all of this, you're not alone.

With God's help, in my own tear-filled wrestling through this message, I have found a way forward. A way to truly love others without losing the best of who I am.

I want to acknowledge up front that this journey of setting and keeping healthy boundaries won't always be easy. We'll have to examine some hard places of dysfunction, distress, and even

Where there is an abundance of chaos, there is usually a lack of good boundaries.

distrust. We'll have to commit to wake up each day with a renewed commitment to assess our boundaries and how we're going to be sure to adhere to them with equal measures of grace, love, and compassion . . . for ourselves and for the ones we're in relationship with.

Compassion is really important to me when I'm processing boundaries. When we're in a difficult relationship or even one that isn't sustainable, especially if addictions are involved, there does need to be a measure of compassion. Because sometimes what is actually driving unhealthy behaviors in people is underlying shame or a lack of peace deep inside. Many times it's both.

What I'm not saying is that because of compassion we condone or enable their actions and stay in situations where there's harm being done. But what I am saying is that, as we take a step back, we can consider having compassion for whatever caused the original root of shame and chaos in their heart that then drove them to try to act and react in such unhealthy ways. We don't want the hurt they've caused to make us betray who we really are. We aren't cruel or mean-spirited so we don't want to bring any of that into our boundary setting.

I also want to have compassion because I don't have life so figured out that I never act and react in unhealthy ways. I have my own issues that I need to work on and work through with counseling. And certainly learning to have compassion appropriately, while still also having boundaries, continues to be one of my biggest lessons.

So if you're ready to work through this, and I mean really work through all of this, then I am too. We're in this together, and there's no one else I'd rather have by my side as we press in and make progress toward the healing and health our hearts are desperately aching for.

And with that I think I'll take a deep breath and go grab another cup of coffee. With great hope in my heart, I'll tuck my Bible under my arm as I walk alongside you.

A note from my counselor, Jim, on triggers:

There are two types of triggers: internal and external. A trigger is a stimulation caused either by an internal thought or an external action from someone else. Whether internal or external, the trigger causes a reaction that makes a painful incident from the past feel as if it's happening in the present. It's almost as if we've been transported back to the "scene of the crime."

The "feeling" part of our brain (known as the limbic system) is wired to search for safety and confidence in what the future holds. In other words, the brain is trying to predict what will happen next.

So, a trigger makes you anxious because it sets off an alarm, making you feel something isn't right or safe.

But the trigger is not the main issue—the main issue is the unhealed trauma still inside you. When you get triggered, it's pointing either to something from your past not yet healed inside you or a new trauma happening in the present moment.

If a fresh trauma is happening and you're in immediate danger, your desire will be to get to safety. If the trigger is because of past trauma, we can learn how to not get hijacked by the anxiety. This will require you to go into your past to work on what's still not healed, while also staying grounded. Stop.

Take a breath and say, "I know what's going on here. I've been here before. I'm not in immediate danger. There is a way out and I can seek help. I can let this feeling inform me, but I don't have to spiral into panic."

And no matter the trigger, always remember you have the power to rise in resiliency. When things around you get out of control, you can call a time-out. You can remove yourself. You can seek others to help you process. You can get a plan. You can schedule something on your calendar to look forward to. All these things will help you avoid spinning in the unsafe feelings and circumstances that are causing you pain and confusion.

Now, Let's Live This . . .

REMEMBER:

- You cannot build trust that keeps getting broken.
- We must not confuse the good commands to love and forgive with the bad realities of enabling and covering up things that are not honoring to God.
- Health cannot bond with unhealth.
- All relationships can be difficult at times, but they should not be destructive to our well-being.
- Boundaries aren't just a good idea, they are a God idea.
- Where there is an abundance of chaos, there is usually a lack of good boundaries.
- It's not unchristian to require people to treat you in healthy ways.

RECEIVE:

"I made the sand a boundary for the sea,
   an everlasting barrier it cannot cross.
The waves may roll, but they cannot prevail;
   they may roar, but they cannot cross it." (Jeremiah 5:22)

REFLECT:

- Describe what you think when you read this: you cannot build trust that keeps getting broken.
- In what ways have you believed it was unchristian to require others to treat you in healthy ways?

PRAYER:

Heavenly Father, when the person who hurts me doesn't see the heartbreak, tears, or emotions they are causing, I know You do. You remind me that I am seen and loved. I am not walking alone. As I start the journey of discovering how boundaries are not just a human idea, but Your idea, I know You will guide me every step of the way. Keep my heart tender and humble while at the same time steadfast and open to all You reveal to me. Continue to show me what You have for me personally in the pages ahead. In Jesus' name, amen.

CHAPTER 2

Naming the Tension That We've All Been Wrestling With

I didn't know what to do anymore. No matter how much I wanted this friendship to work, it wasn't working. Parts of it were good. But then the parts that weren't working were happening over and over. I was spending so much emotional energy trying to avoid another issue that it was becoming increasingly challenging to even enjoy the good times. We had been friends since we were kids, but our lives had gone in dramatically different directions.

It was like going to the beach, looking forward to walking in the sand. There is something so soothing about that for me. But when I step on a sand spur, it stings and momentarily disrupts the beauty of the beach. After hopping around and removing the spur, I walk a little more cautiously for the next couple of steps, but I can still completely enjoy being there. If, however, the beach sand was filled with spurs, I would stop expecting the sand to be soothing and instead get laser-focused on avoiding getting hurt. The beach still looks beautiful. The sand still looks so promising. But if the realities of that sand prove to be hurtful, it's only reasonable at some point to have more realistic expectations. If the spurs aren't removed from the sand, then walking on the beach will not be a peaceful experience. This seems so obvious with sand spurs.

It was much less obvious in this friendship. I knew there were spurs. I knew the spurs would hurt. But instead of acknowledging that the pain was caused by the presence of spurs, I kept mentally beating myself up for being too sensitive. I can't imagine telling someone who stepped on a sand spur that the problem was her feet. And yet I was doing that to myself when hard relational dynamics hurt my heart.

And then other times I would get so angry and frustrated that I would try to solve the issue by removing the individual spurs from the sand. Never realizing that spurs are what carry the seeds that make more of the original plant. In other words, spurs multiply. Spurs not only won't go away on their own, but they tend to just get worse and worse. The source must be addressed.

It had taken me a long time to admit that.

At first, like I said, I just thought the problem was me. Why was I getting so frustrated? I thought I needed to work on my patience. So, I did. But things didn't get better. So, I thought I needed to work on my expectations. Maybe they were too high? Then I found out that expectations are sometimes simmering resentments in disguise. Ouch. So, I changed my phraseology from "expectations" to "needs and desires." That helped, until it didn't.

Then I thought maybe I was spending too much time with my friend. But when I tried to back off a bit, I was told I was giving too little and acting disconnected. Then I tried to do what she said she needed but her needs were constantly changing. And what about my needs? I couldn't figure out how to bring up some of my concerns.

When I tried to explain that some things needed to change, even my best points came out wrong. It had all sounded so rational in my head before the conversation, but then the emotion of the moment made me sound so off. I couldn't keep up with the mental gymnastics. So, I wound up apologizing and regretting I'd brought any of this up.

The spurs weren't just something I was stepping on occasionally. Now they were sticking to me regularly and pricking my heart even after I'd left the beach.

It all just kept swirling in my mind. I kept telling myself it was possible to figure this out. I bounced from feeling angry with my friend to angry with myself. And then things would get a little better. When things were good, they were really good. When they were nice, they were so nice. When they were fun, they were lots of fun.

But then an expectation she had would arise during a phone call or a lunch together or even in a simple text exchange, and I would know the cycle of chaos was about to return. It was as if I'd never tried to address any of this in the first place.

Good, great, confusing, worse, much worse. Feeling bad about myself. Feeling bad about her. Not wanting to feel at all. Staring at the ceiling. Good again, great again, confusing again, worse again, and much worse again. Feeling even worse about myself. Feeling even worse about her. Not wanting to feel at all on even greater levels. Staring at the ceiling. On and on it went. For years.

I finally had to realize that to continue to try and solve the problem *was* part of the problem. Albert Einstein is reported to have said, "If I were given one hour to save the planet, I would spend 59 minutes defining the problem and one minute resolving it." I was doing the opposite. I was spending so much time trying to resolve the individual issues that I'd never properly defined the overarching problem.

The problem wasn't that I had needs and desires that weren't getting met. My friend probably did as well. It wasn't even that we didn't try to talk about each of our needs and desires. The real issue was I started to resent the amount of emotional access to my life I had given to her. If you are a highlighting kind of person, swipe some yellow across that word *access*. It's a big one. It's especially big if we are knee deep in a close relationship and we start feeling unheard, unsafe, uncared for, taken advantage of, or made to pay consequences for choices that we had no control over.

We know access must be carefully protected with so many other things in our lives.

We know this with our homes, cars, bank accounts, social media accounts, and even the streaming accounts we use to watch movies. We have keys. We have passwords. It would never be wise to grant access to others without first being sure that they would be appropriately responsible with that access. I've never heard someone say, "She is so selfish and unchristian for not freely giving out her keys and passwords to her whole neighborhood." Just because someone lives close by doesn't mean we can assume they will be responsible with complete access.

If we give a neighbor a key to our front door, it's because we trust they understand how to be responsible with that kind of access. And if there is an indication that our neighbor isn't being responsible with the access we've given them, we know restricting that access is wise.

I haven't been as wise about understanding how to guard my heart. Maybe this has been a problem for many of us.

Proverbs 4:23 says, "Above all else, guard your heart, for everything you do flows from it." I've often heard this verse taught in the context of dating relationships and purity. But I think it also applies to guarding the access to our hearts in other relationships as well. Interestingly, the Hebrew word for guard, *mišmār*, communicates an active nature of how someone should guard.[1] What this means is that guarding is active, not passive. We aren't trying to protect ourselves *from* love. If we love, we will risk being hurt. But we are trying to protect ourselves *for* love. We don't want to get so consumed with the pain and chaos of unhealthy relationship patterns that we become a carrier of human hurt rather than a conduit of God's love.

Love can be unconditional but relational access never should be. God loves us but He has established that sin causes separation from Him. When Adam and Eve sinned, they were no longer given the same kind of access. What started out as a lot of access to God, with one boundary in the garden of Eden, changed because of sin. And as I keep reading through the Bible, the more the sins of humanity increased, the more the access was decreased, and the more boundaries were given. In Genesis chapter 2 there was one boundary, but as we near the end of the Law and Prophets there are 613.[2]

Then, as we keep reading through the Bible, the access to God became more restricted and conditional. His love was unconditional but access to Him was not.

Here are some important scriptures to consider:

> Surely the arm of the LORD is not too short to save,
> nor his ear too dull to hear.
> But your iniquities have separated
> you from your God;
> your sins have hidden his face from you,
> so that he will not hear. (Isaiah 59:1–2)

> If I had cherished iniquity in my heart,
> the Lord would not have listened. (Psalm
> 66:18 ESV)

> Love can be unconditional
> but relational access
> never should be.

Notice that the words *sin* and *iniquity* are both used in these verses. I am more familiar with sin but not as much with iniquity.

As I studied this, I discovered iniquity points to the character or motivation of the action more than the action itself. So, it's not just what someone does or doesn't do; it's what her actions represent. I think this is where things can get so confusing when we know something someone is doing is hurtful to us, but we can't pinpoint it as sin. It may even contribute to our relationship feeling a little "off"—like something isn't quite right. That's why I'm so grateful the Bible also addresses iniquity, which gets into the nuances of hurtful issues within human relationships that don't clearly point to sin. Reread the verses above and notice that both sin and iniquity have consequences that change the access God allows in His relationships.

What we are looking for are patterns of hurtful and harmful behavior. A hurtful statement can be called a mistake. But a repeated pattern of hurtful statements or uncaring attitudes or even unjust expectations is much more than a mistake. These patterns are misuses of the purposes of a relationship. Why is this so crucial to understand? Because unchecked misuse of a relationship can quickly turn into abuse in a relationship.

A recent Christianity.com article I came across sums up this dangerous progression so well: "Continued iniquity leads to irregular desires, which leads to a degenerate mind. Romans 1:28–32 describes this deviation in graphic detail."[3] When I turned in my Bible to look at what this passage said, I was shocked at what this progression can actually lead to:

> Unchecked misuse of a
> relationship can quickly turn
> into abuse in a relationship.

Furthermore, just as they did not think it worthwhile to retain the knowledge of God, so God gave them over to a depraved mind, so that they do what ought not to be done. They have become filled with every kind of wickedness, evil, greed and depravity. They are full of envy, murder, strife, deceit and malice. They are gossips, slanderers, God-haters, insolent, arrogant and boastful; they invent ways of doing evil; they disobey their parents; they have no understanding, no fidelity, no love, no mercy. Although they know God's righteous decree that those who do such things deserve death, they not only continue to do these very things but also approve of those who practice them.

I know this is heavy stuff. And you may be thinking, "Whoa, Lysa, I'm just trying to figure out a few wonky relationship dynamics. I don't really want to get into all this iniquity and sin stuff." I can feel that way too. But it's crucial to understand how this plays out on a biblical level so we can properly guard our hearts.

Like I said before, boundaries aren't just a good idea, they are a God idea.

We've already talked about how God established boundaries from the very beginning. But what about an example of God using boundaries to guard access? When the temple was constructed, those given the greatest access (the high priests) were also called to the highest standard of purity and responsibility necessary to enter the holy of holies. If they violated God's established boundary and entered the holy of holies without being properly cleansed and purified, death was the consequence.

When Jesus came to make atonement for our sins, we were forgiven, *and* we are also required to live lives where forgiveness is given and received in our relationships with others. Ongoing and unrepented sins still have consequences. God offers all people love, but not all people will have access to life in eternity with Him. Why? Because sin separates. So, if we never repent of our sins and accept the new hearts that come through salvation in Christ, the wages of sin are eternal separation from God.

With all of this in mind, sin and iniquity not only cause separation with God but between people as well.

Like God, we must require from people the responsibility necessary to grant the amount of access we allow them to have in our lives. Too much access without the correct responsibility is detrimental.

Please reread that last sentence and let it soak in. That is the tension we've all been wrestling with in relationships, that we've never quite been able to put our finger on—granting too much access without the correct level of responsibility.

But think of how much clarity we could have by just asking ourselves these questions: Have we required people to be responsible with the amount of access we've granted them? And, do we have the appropriate consequences in place to help hold them accountable if they violate our boundaries?

If we've given them level-ten access but they are only willing or capable of level-three responsibility, that's the real source of the problem. The mistake I've made is trying to get the other person to increase their responsibility. And if they refuse, I've just felt so stuck.

Now, instead of feeling stuck because I can't control the choices of the other person, I take control of reducing the access to the level of responsibility they are capable of. That solution is called a boundary.

> Like God, we must require from people the responsibility necessary to grant the amount of access we allow them to have in our lives.

Setting a boundary is being responsible enough to reduce the access we grant to others based on their ability to be responsible with that access. People who are irresponsible with our hearts should not be granted great access to our hearts. And the same is true for all other kinds of access as well—physical, emotional, spiritual, and financial.

For example, we are a very close-knit family, and my girls and I love sharing clothes. But we've had to establish a new policy around access to our closets. Well, level 10 (complete) access wasn't working and led to a lot of frustration when something went missing or came back damaged. Now, if we want to wear something, we send a text asking to borrow an item and stating when it will be returned. So, the level of access to each other's closets had to be adjusted with these implemented guidelines to maintain respect and, ultimately, keep our dynamics healthy.

Or, maybe you have a friend you spend a lot of time with and you give her details about hard situations you are walking through. But, over and over, she slips and shares those details you didn't want shared with others. The more this happens, the more unsafe you start to feel. Even when you address the problem, it still happens. So, if you don't want details shared, you'll have to reduce the access you give to the more private aspects of your life. This may include deciding ahead of time what topics you are willing to talk about when you get together and not deviating from that decision in a moment of vulnerability.

People who are irresponsible

with our hearts should

not be granted great

access to our hearts.

— *ups*

Or, maybe in your marriage you've trusted your spouse to pay your car insurance bill each quarter. But then on vacation, both of your phones are suddenly bombarded with urgent calls that your insurance is about to get dropped due to delinquent payments. After a serious conversation about what could have happened had the insurance been canceled, and the fact that other bills have been late, too, you both realize you should assume a more active role in bill paying. Obviously, this isn't a deal breaker in your overall trust within your marriage, but it does shed light on the reality that a shift needs to be made so tensions don't continue to rise in this area. It's not that your spouse can't access accounts, but because they were irresponsible with bill paying, safeguards need to be put in place where they are no longer in charge of paying the bills. That's reduced access. Ultimately, you may both decide it's better for you to step back in and schedule the household payments. Then your spouse would be free to grow and excel and exhibit responsibility in other areas.

Bottom line: God established boundaries to protect intimacy, not decimate it. And we should do the same. How to do this appropriately is what this entire message is about.

As we close this chapter, I want you to know three things. First, you are not alone in your struggles. I haven't met even one person who has truly mastered all that we've been talking about. You aren't a relationship failure just because you have relational hardships. You are full of potential and so are those you are in relationship with.

Second, I know part of what makes this complicated is that usually by the time we realize we need boundaries, we are carrying hurt. I want to acknowledge your hurt just like I want others to acknowledge mine. While we want to acknowledge the pain, we don't want to use any part of this message to perpetuate more pain. Boundaries aren't meant to be weaponized. They are meant to be used to prioritize keeping relationships safe.

And last, there is a big difference between difficult relationships and destructive relationships. We will address this important distinction in later chapters, but if you are being abused, please get help immediately from safe, trained professionals.

If the problems in your relationships look more like hurricanes than sand spurs, be honest about that. That's why sometimes we need good boundaries and sometimes we need goodbyes. We will leave space in this book for both to be acknowledged and addressed.

You and I are going to make it through this, friend. And in the end, we will be more equipped and eager to love others without betraying ourselves in the process. That's the best way to honor God's design for love. And that's really what all this is about.

A note from Jim on access

Allowing someone access without accountability will eventually lead to abandonment. If I give you unlimited access to me and there's no accountability, either I'm going to leave the relationship, or you will. If someone perpetually acts out, that person *has* abandoned the relationship. Remember: If you don't have clear rules—if you don't set boundaries for the relationship—then you'll be ruled by the other person. You just may not know it.

Now, Let's Live This . . .

REMEMBER:

- Love can be unconditional but relational access never should be.
- Unchecked misuse of a relationship can quickly turn into abuse in a relationship.
- Like God, we must require from people the responsibility necessary to grant the amount of access we allow them to have in our lives.
- People who are irresponsible with our hearts should not be granted great access to our hearts.

RECEIVE:

Above all else, guard your heart,
for everything you do flows from it. (Proverbs 4:23)

Furthermore, just as they did not think it worthwhile to
retain the knowledge of God, so God gave them over
to a depraved mind, so that they do what ought not to
be done. They have become filled with every kind of
wickedness, evil, greed and depravity. They are full
of envy, murder, strife, deceit and malice. They are
gossips, slanderers, God-haters, insolent, arrogant and
boastful; they invent ways of doing evil; they disobey
their parents; they have no understanding, no fidelity,
no love, no mercy. Although they know God's righteous
decree that those who do such things deserve death,
they not only continue to do these very things but also
approve of those who practice them. (Romans 1:28–32)

REFLECT:

- Explain this concept in your own words: "Love can be unconditional but relational access never should be."
- What might it look like if you were to require the level of responsibility from others that matches the amount of access you've given them?

PRAYER:

God, as I process the relationships that have caused hurt in my life, keep my heart turned toward You. Remind me that boundaries are meant to protect intimacy, not decimate it. Father, I hand You my deepest fears and anxieties because of my difficult relationships. I trust You to lead me with clarity in the right direction. Thank You for everything You're revealing to me personally right now. In Jesus' name, amen.

CHAPTER 3

It's Not About the Problems, It's About What the Problems Represent

Relationships often die not because of conversations that were had but rather conversations that were needed but never had.

Conversations open the way for us to address what is and isn't working. But even more, they help us establish healthy patterns instead of accepting patterns that are unhealthy. On a continuum, relationships are either constructive on one end or destructive on the other. Here's how I wrote this out in my journal:

HEALTHY   **DYSFUNCTIONAL**

Constructive ◀ Enhancing–Fulfilling–Indifferent/Stagnant–Difficult–Damaging ▶ Destructive

> Relationships often die not because of conversations that were had but rather conversations that were needed but never had.

Obviously, there are many other words that express the different degrees along that relationship continuum. But there is something that will always move us in the negative direction of difficult to damaging to destructive.

The issue is dysfunction.

And can I just admit right up front here . . . that isn't a word I have dared to use much with past relationship issues. Saying "dysfunction" used to feel so offensive it immediately put me on the defensive. But now, I've learned to simply let it sit in front of me, to tilt my head and dare myself to consider some things. Confession: I have dysfunctions. Other people I know have dysfunctions. Alive humans have dysfunctions. It shouldn't scare us when we acknowledge that dysfunctions exist. But we should be concerned when someone lives as if dysfunctions are normal.

Being aware of our dysfunctions doesn't fix them. If we want healthier relationships we must also be willing to address them.

Ahem. I'm pointing at myself here.

I'm reminded of a time when my sister came to visit. We'd just finished a few renovations where some of the wiring in our house had to be reworked. For some reason our hot water heater would no longer work unless the back floodlights of our house were turned on. So, if you were enjoying your hot shower and someone turned off the floodlights—*wham!*—cold water was very quickly making you cringe, scream, and yell downstairs for someone to turn the floodlights back on.

Now, I totally get what you're probably thinking. Surely I called an electrician right away to come and repair this very obvious and alarming wiring dysfunction, right?!

You would think. But no.

I just made a mental note to remind all my guests that the back floodlights must be on, both day and night, for them to have a hot shower. I educated my family on our reality. I even considered making a little sign for the bathrooms.

Hello, dysfunction.

My sister tilted her head and said, "Lysa, you know that's weird, right? You do know an electrician would be able to fix that, right?"

Yes and no.

Technically, I guess I knew an electrician could fix the problem. But that wasn't my automatic response. Calling an electrician would cost money. Money, that as children growing up, we didn't have. So, this thought process got ingrained in me that it's better to get scrappy and navigate around problems rather than to pay to fix them.

Nothing tragic happened when I was getting hot water in this strange way.

But this isn't just about floodlights and hot water. It's about what the floodlights and hot water situation represents.

It's about no longer being aware of just how dysfunctional things have become and reacting as if something is normal when it absolutely is not. Dysfunction means things aren't working correctly. In other words, something gets in the way of how things ought to be. For example, a mother is supposed to parent her child. But it is a dysfunction when a child has to parent the mother. Another example is when a spouse is expected not just to be a partner but a savior of the other spouse. Or when one friend's happiness is dependent on another friend making them feel okay all the time.

But in relationships we also must consider the part that distortion plays within the dysfunctions that play out. I love how Luis Villareal comments on the connection between dysfunction and distortion:

> Because of the Fall (Gen. 2–3), all of us have some level of distortion or dysfunction. We do not perceive, think, feel, or behave in the healthiest way possible at all times. As a result, emotional distortions such as latent anxiety, shame, low self-esteem, pessimism, depression, and perfectionism (among others) dynamically interact and affect marriage and family interactions.[1]

And I would add, these distortions can affect all relationships. Distortions of reality feed dysfunctions. Our personal issues don't magically go away in relationships. Often, our lack of self-awareness collide with the other person's lack of self-awareness, and we have a choice to make. We can use this conflict to make us more aware of our issues or totally ignore what the other person is saying and stay wrongly convinced that this will get better on its own. But it won't. Appropriately addressing the issue is healthy. Ignoring the issue increases the likelihood of dysfunction.

In a relationship when truth is manipulated, denied, or partially omitted for the sake of covering up behaviors that should be addressed, dysfunctions may not just be difficult, they may become destructive. We then run the risk of a pattern of wrongs being tolerated as acceptable, because over time they start to feel less alarming, more acceptable, and eventually our version of "normal."

And while the issues with my hot water were more of an inconvenience, the dysfunctions hiding out in my relationships and life could be truly detrimental. I've made the mistake of spending countless amounts of emotional energy on trying to please other people—even when I shouldn't have. I've tried to

Distortions of reality
feed dysfunctions.

fix other people. I've tried to change myself to accommodate others and avoid conflicts. I've taken on other people's issues as if they were mine to own and felt noble about how loyal I am. I've assumed other people had the same definitions about how to care for the relationship, how to care for one another, and how to take care of issues that arise. But worst of all, I have betrayed myself by knowing something was off in a relationship but letting that person convince me otherwise.

Remember in the last chapter when I said that I finally realized I had begun to resent the amount of access I had given my friend? Let's define what I mean by "access" a little more. It wasn't that I was resenting my friend or even our friendship. It was that I was resenting what this friendship was doing to me. I had allowed her to have such a prominent place in my heart and mind that her words and actions carried a lot of weight. So much so, that when she was irresponsible with what she said or did it really affected my well-being. This revealed for me personally that I had some codependent tendencies I hadn't realized. In other words, if she wasn't okay with me, I was having a hard time being okay with me.

The closeness we shared started to feel unsafe when she seemed eager to label me with her opinions instead of really listening to me and helping me process what I was going through. I started walking away from almost every conversation feeling wrongly judged and misunderstood, and regretting sharing my struggles with her. She would call it "holding me accountable to being a good Christian" but through counseling I started to see this wasn't her true intention. She was actually holding me hostage to doing things her way or she would make her disapproval known not just to me but to others as well. And, in the end, I realized I had given too much access to her without requiring that same level of responsibility from her.

That was a good revelation. However, just realizing this wasn't enough. I had to take action.

So, how do we define and determine the responsibilities we've been talking so much about?

In the midst of trying to figure this out, a friend sent me this verse: "A friend loves at all times, and a brother is born for a time of adversity. One who has no sense shakes hands in pledge and puts up security for a neighbor" (Proverbs 17:17–18).

At first blush I thought verse 17 was only about how friends are there for you in the good times, but a blood relationship is there no matter if the times are good or bad. However, what this verse can also mean is that there are some friends who are there for you in both good times and times of adversity to the extent that they become as close to you as family.

This kind of emotional closeness encourages that each of you grants great access to one another. And that is not a bad thing. However, with such closeness or access, you must understand what each of you needs from the other to continue a mutually healthy and respectful relationship. This is what I've been referring to when I say we need someone's level of responsibility to match their level of access. You get to communicate what makes you feel respected and disrespected; safe and unsafe; healthy and unhealthy. Your definition of this determines what you need from your closest people. For me, this requires:

- trust
- truthfulness
- transparency

- tenderness, and
- a team approach where we can hold each other accountable and hold each other close at the same time.

Use my list above to help think through what responsible access means to you.

After processing through this for myself, I think what would have helped with the friend I mentioned is if she had been more transparent about her own struggles. If she had shared her problems instead of just criticizing me, it could have paved the way for more tenderness in our conversations. We might have felt more like two friends, both with struggles, helping each other without condemnation.

Now, let's go back to the Proverbs 17 passage we were just in and look at verse 18. At first, it seems to be disconnected and possibly contradictory to verse 17. As in, be there for your friend "at all times," until she's in a financial situation and you need to cosign her car loan, and then you run. But this isn't meant as a harsh contradiction . . . nor is it just about finances. The example here is about a financial pledge but we can apply this principle to other issues of equal importance. The people in biblical culture would very much relate to the irresponsible risk of taking on the financial debt of someone else to the detriment of you or your family.

Derek Kidner, a respected Old Testament scholar, pointed out that verses 17 and 18 work together. It is understandable to want to help out a close friend, but it is not wise to refuse to apply responsibility and reason to this relationship. Otherwise, it could become "a blind guarantee which may lead the recipient to rashness, and both to ruin."[2]

Pay close attention to the phraseology in verse 18: "One who has no sense shakes hands in pledge and puts up security for a neighbor."

The "no sense" or "blind guarantee" as mentioned above isn't

Good relationships

require good boundaries.

— ups

just addressing the foolish person. It's also addressing a person who is wise but isn't being wise in a relationship. They are lacking the application of good judgment, which can happen to all of us, especially when our emotions are deeply invested in a relationship. "While it sometimes can be very hard to say 'no' to people who want help, an unwise agreement is still an unwise agreement even if it is difficult to decline getting involved."[3]

In the same way, allowing unwise access is still unwise even if it is difficult to draw a boundary.

So, what I really want us to take away here is how crucial it is to require appropriate responsibility and to apply reason to all our relationships. We don't throw reason out of our relationships. We apply reason to our relationships. And then we can cultivate responsible relationships.

And isn't that what we all want? Good relationships require good boundaries. And in the next chapter we will discover that good boundaries require appropriate consequences. This is all about pursuing good for you, me, and all our relationships. Now, if you'll excuse me, I'm off to call my electrician.

A note from Jim on identifying dysfunction

1. It's important to be able to take an honest look at the current dysfunction. It's often helpful to have a counselor or another wise person help you see what you may not be able to see or name for yourself. Proverbs 20:5 says, "The purposes of a person's heart are deep waters, but one who has insight draws them out."

2. Sometimes you'll need to explore your family of origin dynamics, childhood experiences, and more. This includes assessing both the facts and the impact of your life story. Remember to name, not blame, anyone who was involved in your past. A safe place to do this is with a professional counselor who knows how to help you better understand how the rules you grew up under and the roles you were required to play affected you and may be leading you to call normal some things that are dysfunctional.

3. Consider these questions:
   - Where am I out of alignment with what I *want* to be true about my life and what is *actually* true?
   - Where am I carrying an unusual amount of relational stress in my life? (Think about where your mouth is saying yes but your body or emotional capacity is saying no.)
   - Am I trying to numb relational pain in my life?
   - Do I feel the need to cover up or minimize behaviors by someone in my family because that's just what we do?
   - Where in my life am I out of alignment with my personal values?

Now, Let's Live This . . .

REMEMBER:

- Relationships often die not because of conversations that were had but rather conversations that were needed but never had.
- Distortions of reality feed dysfunctions.
- Where truth is manipulated, denied, or partially omitted for the sake of covering up behaviors that should be addressed, dysfunctions may not just be difficult, they may become destructive.
- We need a person's level of responsibility to match their level of access.
- Good relationships require good boundaries.

RECEIVE:

A friend loves at all times,
    and a brother is born for a time of adversity.
One who has no sense shakes hands in pledge
    and puts up security for a neighbor. (Proverbs 17:17–18)

REFLECT:

- As you read this chapter, what conversations came to mind that you may need to initiate with the people in your life? Don't try to initiate all the conversations at the same time. Prioritize the top three you know are most important to have sooner rather than later. Schedule them with time in between to process, pray, and get to a good place emotionally.
- "Good relationships require good boundaries." List some good boundaries you already have in place in your relationships.

PRAYER:

God, help me not avoid or become numb to the dysfunction that may be present in some of my relationships. Even when naming it, addressing it, or confronting it feels overwhelming or even impossible, remind me that I am not alone. You are with me. Give me the courage to have the conversations I need to have. Give me wisdom and discernment so I stay soft enough to give the right people the right access but firm enough to reduce the access I've given to people who aren't responsible or trustworthy. In Jesus' name, amen.

CHAPTER 4

God Takes Boundary Violations Very Seriously and So Should We

Sometimes boundaries work. And other times they don't.

I'm going to make a few admissions that I'm not very proud of. Sometimes my boundaries don't work. And it's because of me. Here's why:

- I have been more concerned with tending to other people's needs to the point I don't always know what I need. I remember, with one of the worst betrayals I've ever experienced, hugging the person and telling them what they needed at that moment was what was most important. And then I went into the bathroom and hyperventilated.
- I have rewarded people for disrespecting my boundaries. A

classic line I've used: "But they didn't mean it this time. I'll just love them better and things will get better."

- I hint around at setting a boundary rather than clearly stating it. If I am not convinced of my limits and how damaging it is for someone to push me past my limits, I'll be weak communicating my boundaries. If I don't take my need for a boundary seriously, I can't expect other people to take me seriously enough to respect my boundary.
- I wrongly believe someone's pushback is an indication that I'm doing something wrong. I don't like the drama and complications that can happen when I establish a boundary and the other person continues to ask things of me that aren't in alignment with that boundary. Or they just flat-out ignore the boundary. And when they do, my natural inclination is to take the blame.
- I allow myself to get pulled into debates about the boundary. My counselor has often reminded me, "Adults inform. Children explain." I forget this. And when I do, I feel as if I have to prove that I'm not doing anything wrong by setting a boundary. At times I've been convinced by the other person that the boundary is the real problem and things will never get better while the boundary is in place.
- Sometimes I can't find the strength to stand firm with people who know both me and the person with whom I've set a boundary. When other people excuse away or minimize this person's behavior, keeping the boundary can feel doubly difficult. If others don't feel personally threatened or triggered by this person's behavior, then they may accuse me of making more out of this situation than I "should." Usually, these are people who feel a little inconvenienced or frustrated by the boundary and would rather I ignore the issues at hand than address them. This can often happen at the holidays when

your family wants everyone to get together, but you have a necessary boundary with someone whose behavior you are no longer willing to tolerate. Or it can happen at work when you are expected to "set aside personal issues" but sometimes professional issues cross over into personal violations.

On top of all that, sometimes my emotional wiring also plays into my resistance to keeping boundaries. I am wired to want peace. I want everyone to be calm, happy, and stable. Anything that seems to disrupt peace bothers me. So, if someone is aggravated or angry or even acting in a way that makes me doubt my boundary, I can be tempted to give in. Drop the boundary. Forget the consequence. Reestablish someone's level of access without remembering the need for them to be responsible. It's like I have temporary amnesia and start thinking the *boundary* is hindering peace instead of remembering the boundary is the only fighting chance we have at reclaiming our peace.

Trust me with this. If someone is demanding you drop a boundary or trying to charm and convince you that it's no longer necessary—beware. People who are genuine and honest don't go on and on trying to convince you what a good person they are. Proverbs 31:30 reminds us that "charm is deceptive."

I know all this. And still, sometimes I can so desperately want things to be better that I try to reframe reality and convince myself that the person has changed when they haven't. My confusion or exhaustion, or my compassion, can make me want to give in.

Even when the reality of life screams no. Even when I know I'm rescuing, and I shouldn't be. Even when it hurts me. Even when it's unhealthy for me. Even when, based on past experiences, I know saying yes in the short term will cause extremely hard dynamics in the long term.

Still, I find myself giving in.

And when I do give in, the boundary I'd worked so hard to establish becomes nothing more than a passive suggestion or a threat I never intended to keep. Ugh. Then I'm not just frustrated by that person's lack of respect—I'm doubly frustrated by my own inability to respect myself.

When we allow a boundary to be violated, bad behavior will be validated.

This is the cycle of *bad boundary-setting*: I know a change is needed. I set a boundary with a consequence. But if my motivation is to control, manipulate, or punish another person, I'm already setting myself up for failure. And even if my boundary has the right motivation to better control myself, if I don't have consequences established for boundary violations, I'll never enforce those consequences. So, the boundary is violated. I don't enforce the consequences. The boundary is violated again. I'm aggravated but again I don't enforce the consequences. The other person keeps pushing. I want to believe it will be better this time, so I give in and drop the boundary. The bad behavior isn't better and often gets worse over time. Simmering resentments develop in my heart. Now I'm not just frustrated—I'm angry. I say things I shouldn't say. I do things I wouldn't normally do. I get into the crazy cycle of trying to get the person to change, and eventually the situation becomes so exacerbating I not only *give in* I *give up.*

And, in the end, I feel like such a failure because it seems like I couldn't make the boundary work. Or I just forever think poorly of the other person and label them with words like *jerk, ridiculous, full of themselves, crazy, impossible, too much, too demanding, too sensitive, too overwhelming,* or *too selfish.* Every future thought of them is then based on the worst experiences I had with them. Then it's just awkward when that person's name comes up. I bite my tongue but inside there's a whole lot that could spew out.

None of this is healthy. Not for me. Not for them. Not for the

> # When we allow a boundary to be violated, bad behavior will be validated.

other people around us. This is when we can easily start to simmer in resentments that will boil over at some point. And, as we already established, the absence of boundaries means the presence of chaos.

So, like I said, sometimes boundaries don't work—because of me and my approach. It's important for me to own this and then do the hard work of changing the way I think about boundaries. And this *is* hard work. It's worthy work, but it isn't easy. If you relate to any of the above, I want to fully acknowledge along with you that all of this can sound much tidier to read about than to actually apply. That's why throughout this journey we need to keep remembering that *good* boundaries originated with God and are modeled by God. We will have so much more confidence in how to handle a boundary violation when we feel validation from God's examples.

God takes boundary violations very seriously. And so should we. In Genesis chapter 2, we see evidence of just how important boundaries are when God gave Adam and Eve the one boundary of not eating from the tree of the knowledge of good and evil. Here are some important facts we should pay attention to:

Boundaries define and protect freedom. When God gave the boundary, He spoke in the context of freedom. He wasn't trying to be cruel to Adam and Eve. He was trying to protect their freedom. God said to Adam, "You are free to eat from any tree in the garden" (Genesis 2:16) before He communicated the boundary around the one tree they must avoid. God also kept His communication very simple. He defined that they were free to do this, but not that. If you violate this boundary, there's a consequence.

Access requires responsibility. Remember those three words we've talked about before: *access, responsibility,* and *consequence?* Adam and Eve had great access to God and the garden. And they had a great responsibility that came along with that access. In Genesis 2:15, Adam and Eve were told to keep the garden: "The Lᴏʀᴅ God took the man and put him in the garden of Eden to work it and keep it" (ᴇsᴠ). At first glance, we may read this to mean they were to be gardeners and keepers of the garden of Eden. Interestingly, that same word *keep* in Hebrew, *samar,* can also be translated as to "guard" or "protect." It's used of priests guarding and protecting the temple (Numbers 3:38; Numbers 18:7). It's also used of the guards who were to keep watch at the watchtower (Nehemiah 13:22). This helps us see that Adam and Eve in the garden were so much more than just "gardeners." They were guards and protectors of the sacred space that God gave them.[1] The same is true of us. We are to guard and protect our hearts and our minds to make sure we keep good in and evil out. We are to guard and protect our testimony and make sure our lives produce the fruit of God's Spirit in us. And we are to guard and protect our calling to love God and love people. (Note to self: that doesn't say love God and enable people.)

Broken boundaries bring consequences. When Adam and Eve violated the boundary, there were consequences. And one of those consequences was God reducing their access to Him and removing them from the garden. They weren't responsible with their access, so their access was dramatically affected. They weren't responsible with their freedom, so their freedom was affected. They weren't responsible with the one rule God gave them. That made more rules necessary. In Genesis we see that Adam and Eve were given one boundary. By the time we read through the Law and the Prophets we find hundreds of boundaries that God put in place for us "stiff-necked" people (Exodus 32:9, Deuteronomy 9:6; 2 Kings 17:14;

2 Chronicles 30:8; Nehemiah 9:16). He loves us unconditionally and He will not tolerate our sin. Both are true with God and both can be true in our relationships as well. God had grace but His grace was there to lead people to better behavior, not to enable bad behavior. And the same should be true of our grace as well.

Consequences should be for protection not harm. When Adam and Eve were sent out from the garden, they were never allowed to return. As a matter of fact, God put angels at the entry to guard and prevent them from returning. While this may seem cruel or too harsh, there were good and necessary reasons for this boundary to be as distinct as a wall. If Adam and Eve would have been allowed back into the garden, they would have been tempted to eat once again from the other tree in the middle of the garden, called the tree of life. The tree of life would perpetuate their state of being for all eternity. When Adam and Eve were sinless, that was a great thing. But now that they'd eaten from the tree of the knowledge of good and evil, sin had entered in and their beings were no longer perfect. They carried with them the consequences of sin. They were in the process of dying. To eat of the tree of life in that state would have perpetuated them for all eternity in sin, depravity, decay, and therefore eternal separation from God. So, God not only limited but actually prevented Adam and Eve from having access to the garden and the tree of life to protect them—not to be cruel to them. It was the severity of the boundary violation that required the severity of the consequence. We will talk about this more in later chapters. But it is important to keep in mind that the consequence should serve to protect you and, if possible, the relationship—not do more harm. God gave the consequence to Adam and Eve but He didn't abandon them, as we will soon see.

We do want to remember why we need the boundary so we will keep the boundary and its protection in place. It's taken me a long time to realize that each time I establish a boundary and then make exceptions to keeping it, the cycle of chaos tries to suck me back in. If I was unwilling to accept the behavior that caused me to draw the boundary in the first place, it will bother me even more when it resurfaces. Picture a beach ball being held under water. When the external force of keeping it under control in the water is released, the ball doesn't just float to the surface. It explodes. That's a good word picture my counselor, Jim, gave me as I processed all this. Chances are, without a boundary, unless significant healthy changes have been made by the other person, dysfunction will resurface and possibly even explode to the surface.

Healthy changes in someone can't be measured just by the words they speak. There must be evidence of changed thoughts, changed habits, changed behaviors, changed reactions, and changed patterns demonstrated consistently over a long period of time. How long? As long as it takes.

Let me share one more word picture with you that might help you see what we often feel in challenging relationships but have a hard time expressing in words. Changing an outside behavior without changing the internal issue that's driving the behavior is like painting a house that has a crumbling foundation. From the road, the house may look impressive. But if you attempt to live in that dwelling, not only will it be bothersome but over time it could be very dangerous.

A few months ago, Brooke and Nick (my youngest daughter and her husband) were house hunting in a charming neighborhood with older starter homes full of character and curb appeal. If you were willing to put in some sweat equity and invest in renovating, these homes held great potential. The problem was many young couples were attracted to this area, but there were very few houses for sale. Several houses went under contract within hours of coming on the market. Since Brooke and Nick hadn't moved to that town yet, they missed some really good houses because they couldn't get there to see them quickly enough. So, they changed their tactics and decided they would have to put an offer in on the next appealing house after just looking at the photos online.

A few days later, an adorable bungalow went up for sale. I was with them when the pictures showed up on a real estate website and the house looked amazing. Y'all, the charm of this place instantly drew us in, and the price was surprisingly affordable. On the outside, everything was absolutely amazing—the stuff that starter-home dreams are made of!

We all agreed that making an offer was necessary if they wanted to be in the running. Brooke and Nick called the real estate agent, made the offer, and we made plans to see the house the next day. We were pretty bummed when we hadn't heard back from the sellers by the time we got to the house less than twenty-four hours later. And it wasn't ideal that it was pouring rain so we couldn't spend any time looking around the yard. But I encouraged them that looking at a house in the rain is actually a good thing because if there are any water issues, you want to see them before you own them!

Never has a statement been more true than when we walked down to the basement of this adorable-looking home. I've never seen water spraying out from basement walls like I saw that day. We are talking spraying out—like, you could have stood under any one of the leaks and washed your hair and your dog at the same time. Actually, there was so much water, an entire family plus their dogs and grandmas could have all splashed around in that basement.

Brooke and Nick quickly rescinded their offer. No amount of outside charm could make up for the foundational issues that needed to be fixed on the inside. Paint is beautiful unless it is a mask that hides serious underlying issues.

In the same way, changed behaviors are good unless they are a temporary performance with a relapse waiting to happen in the wings. As I mentioned before, Proverbs 31:30 warns us that "charm is deceptive." It's so easy to be charmed into dropping a boundary. We can have a few good days or even a few good months when it seems things are better. But remember, be honest about what's really happening. Don't continue to excuse negative or destructive patterns of behavior or addictions, as if they are just occasional slip-ups and isolated mistakes. There is something deeper going on in the foundational thinking and processing of someone who has been hurting you with their poor choices over and over. "Things are better" is not the same as "things are healed."

If we drop our boundaries too soon, trying to resurrect those boundaries when the chaos returns will become more and more challenging. And the constant charge of devastating emotions will become more and more damaging. Trying to save a relationship by excusing away boundaries is like trying to save a house with a flooded basement by shooting more and more holes into the foundation.

Ask me how I know. Ask me how many nights I've cried myself to sleep, feeling the impossible weight of wanting someone else to cooperate with necessary boundaries only to have them be violated over and over.

Sometimes it takes me a long time to acknowledge reality. And that's certainly been true for me in relationships. Being loyal and hoping things will get better is not a bad trait until hope deferred starts to make my heart sick (Proverbs 13:12).

I posted this question on Instagram the other night: "Why is it that a flag literally has to be on fire before I tilt my head and say it might be red?" If it's red, it's red. If someone's actions toward me are hurting me, they're hurting me. If it's concerning, it's concerning. If it's wrong, it's wrong. And we should be willing to give grace for mistakes. But if the issues are ongoing and continuously harmful, we must acknowledge that and act accordingly. It's not that we don't want to be prayerful and hopeful and eager for positive changes in the other person's life. But we don't want to become so eager and overcommitted to their health that we stay undercommitted to our own.

I know I've said it before, and I'll probably say it many more times (mostly because I have to preach this to my Pollyanna self a lot!)—drawing wise boundaries is me fighting for the relationship. It's for their good and mine! Loosening my boundaries and enabling them to hurt the relationship and harm me isn't helping them. I am not honoring Jesus when I give permission for the other person to act in ways that Jesus never would.

Yes, Jesus laid down His life for sinners. But it wasn't so they could keep sinning. It was for a holy purpose leading to wholeness, healing, and salvation of their souls. Jesus didn't enable people. Jesus didn't beg people. Jesus didn't accept excuses for sin or let people off the hook because they were mostly good. No, He instructed them to leave their lives of sin. (The woman He forgave and rescued from getting stoned—John 8.) He called out the Pharisees for their harsh, demeaning, and judgmental attitudes. (Those hiding their own sin while wanting to stone the woman for her sin—also John 8.) He informed the rich young ruler to give up what was controlling him and holding him back (Matthew 19). Jesus tended to His need to be alone with the Father even when the crowds had needs and demands of Him (Luke 5).

And most telling of all, though Jesus had compassion for all people and offered salvation to all people, those who reject His gift and refuse to acknowledge Him as their Savior will not enter into heaven. There it is again: access requires responsibility. A refusal of that responsibility requires a consequence. This is set up this way for holy and honorable reasons.

So, if we draw a boundary and someone says we aren't "acting like Jesus" we can certainly check ourselves—our tone, our words, and our actions. But remember to consider the source of

> Jesus laid down His life for sinners. But it wasn't so they could keep sinning.

that statement. The problem isn't the boundary, it's that the other person won't respect the boundary.

Before we close this chapter, I want to speak tenderly to your heart. Just you and me. You're going to make it. And so am I. But it's going to get hard. Really hard. I so wish I was standing right with you, whispering a boundaries pep talk into your ear the next time someone hurts you and tries to make you feel like the crazy one. And I wish you were doing the same for me when I need to be reminded of these truths, because I surely will need to be preached to with these very words I've written.

Just a few nights ago, I wish I could have had a little conference call with you. I was crying. A big, ugly, my-eyes-were-swollen-the-next-day cry. I had such hopes that a conversation with someone with whom I'd set boundaries would go well. The boundaries seemed to have worked. I wanted to have more interaction with the person. I'd held strong for so long and they seemed to have been so sincere in their promise that they'd changed. They also committed to being kind and to listen without attacking me if I would be willing to have a face-to-face conversation. So, I agreed.

And it took only about thirty minutes for me to realize what a mistake I'd made.

I was shocked by how things started off okay but then very quickly turned harsh.

I felt so foolish.

I felt scared.

I felt lost in all the confusion swirling in their accusations against me and their grand statements about how much God was with them and that they were praying for my cold heart.

Not one other human who I do daily life with would have agreed with what this person was saying about me, but this person's words still carried such weight that every syllable landed like a dagger straight through my heart.

Then came that moment that I thought to myself, *I'm such an idiot. Boundaries don't work.* But then something amazing happened. Though I was shaking on the inside, I didn't sink down to the level of returning hate for hate. Or accusation for accusation. Instead, I told them that what they were doing was not acceptable and that I would no longer allow them to come to my home until they stopped the harmful behavior.

And it worked.

No, they didn't change on the spot.

No, they didn't acknowledge that what they were doing was unhealthy.

No, they didn't apologize or even recognize how their actions were hurting me.

But the person did leave. And though I cried buckets afterward, I realized I had never lost control of myself in the midst of the confrontation. And that was a huge win.

I'm not a boundaries failure. Neither are you. We are in process. And that, my friend, is one of the healthiest places to be. Remember, boundaries aren't going to fix the other person. But they are going to help you stay fixed on what is good, what is acceptable, and what you need to stay healthy and safe.

I can't be there to whisper all of this in your ear. But I sure will be the friend who understands the next time we get together to process all of this. Love you . . .

Boundaries aren't going to
fix the other person. But they
are going to help you stay
fixed on what is good, what
is acceptable, and what you
need to stay healthy and safe.

— ups

A note from Jim on the difference between good and bad boundaries

Let's take some time to look at the different motivations, mindsets, approaches, and potential outcomes of good and bad boundaries.

Good boundaries = My focus is on what I do

Motivation ➜ Self-control

Mindset ➜ I am responsible for my actions.
- I manage *my* behavior.
- I own the actions I choose.

Approach ➜ I focus on my self-care, safety, sanity, and other things in my life I can control.

Outcome ➜ I accept that I am powerless to control other people. Instead, I use my energy to limit my interactions with difficult people, remove myself from destructive relationships, and pursue loving well the people in my healthy relationships that deserve the best of me.

Bad boundaries = My focus is on what the other person does

Motivation ➜ Controlling or punishing the other person to get what I need

Mindset ➡ I want them to do something different from what they are doing.

- I have to change *their* behavior. Or, I am responsible to help manage their behavior.
- I own the actions they choose.

Approach ➡ Hyper-focused on the other person while constantly negotiating with and trying to motivate (sometimes manipulating) them to do what I feel is right and get from them what I feel I must have.

Outcome ➡ A frustrating cycle of me trying to manage the unmanageable dysfunctions until I'm completely burned out, unhealthy, and bitter. Relationships are no longer a source of satisfaction and fulfillment but instead a constant drain on my always-frazzled emotions.

Ways this can play out in everyday scenarios:

Scenario: Someone from your friend group is posting things on social media that really bother you.

Bad boundary: I tell her if she doesn't stop posting those messages, I'm going to start debating her in the comments and posting things on my social media that publicly correct her.

Good boundary: I can, with love, mention my concerns but not cross over into trying to control what she posts or publicly shame her. If she continues, I can mute her social media account. This may be a better first step than unfollowing her but if unfollowing is more appropriate, then I can make that choice.

Scenario: There's a sharp disagreement between you and a family member.

Bad boundary: I rally other people to my side in order to convince a family member that they must change their attitudes and actions toward me. I feel like if I can get enough other people to agree with me, then we can all put enough pressure on the family member to agree with me.

Good boundary: I focus on what I can do to manage my own emotions and responses to this disagreement. If I need to process with others, I can choose not to engage in conversations that encourage my emotional spiral. Discussing the situation with a few trusted advisors can be healthy. Talking with anyone who only wants the juicy details is slander and will take me into a pit of gossip.

Scenario: A coworker once again asks you to complete a task for them that's become an emergency because they failed to plan.

Bad boundary: Hyperextending myself hoping to be acknowledged by my coworker as the hero while telling them, "I'll help you this time, but if this ever happens again, I won't step in to rescue you." (But the reality is, you already have a pattern of rescuing this person and will likely continue.)

Good boundary: I can predetermine what my response will be so that I will not be pulled into trying to save the situation. For example, "Unfortunately my plate is already full, and I've made the personal commitment not to make my family sacrifice when I take on work that isn't mine to manage." To help prevent me from wavering in my decision, I can put my phone on "do not disturb" on the weekends or during family gatherings so I'm not triggered by work emails or requests from this person.

Scenario: Someone in my small group at church recently betrayed my trust by sharing some things we talked about in confidence.

Bad boundary: I feel pressured to attend my small group tonight even though I'm in a very raw place emotionally. So, I'll call the leader and tell her she has to make sure the environment is safe for me to come and insist she tells the person who broke my trust that they can't do that anymore.

Good boundary: I can address the hurt privately with the person and inform her that I will be taking a break from our small group for a season. Instead of feeling guilty, I remind myself that it's okay not to attend an event or gathering when I sense it's not safe for me to be in the presence of someone who has hurt me or undermined my trust.

Now, Let's Live This . . .

REMEMBER:

- "Adults inform. Children explain." —Jim Cress
- When we allow a boundary to be violated, bad behavior will be validated.
- The absence of boundaries means the presence of chaos.
- The problem isn't the boundary, it's that the other person won't respect the boundary.
- Boundaries aren't going to fix the other person. But they are going to help you stay fixed on what is good, what is acceptable, and what you need to stay healthy and safe.

RECEIVE:

Charm is deceptive, and beauty is fleeting;
> but a woman who fears the Lord is to be praised.
> (Proverbs 31:30)

Hope deferred makes the heart sick,
> but a longing fulfilled is a tree of life. (Proverbs 13:12)

REFLECT:

- Name a time when you unknowingly validated bad behavior by allowing a boundary to be violated. Looking back, how did that make you feel and what did it lead to?
- Dropping boundaries too soon could create major complications and difficult consequences. What are the reasons this could be problematic in your relationships?

PRAYER:

Heavenly Father, Thank You for filling Your Word with truths on how and why to set biblical boundaries. Please continue to reveal Yourself to me as I learn, consider, and process some potentially necessary boundaries I may need to implement in my life. I pray that You would continue to work in me and through me so that I can be the healthiest, most whole, yielded-to-You version of myself. In Jesus' name, amen.

CHAPTER 5

You Are Already Doing This Really Well

I love good smells. A pot roast in the crock pot. The blush pink roses growing in my yard. A newly printed book. An old hymnal. Freshly cut grass. Three drops of lemon and two drops of lavender in my oil diffuser. My favorite candle. Sheets that are still hot from the dryer. Waffles made on a cast iron skillet. An organized office supply store. (An unorganized one just doesn't smell as good. Trust me.) The early morning salt air at the beach. My grandkids lathered in baby lotion.

And when I discover a new smell I like, it's just pure joy to my soul. That brings me to the point of why I'm oversharing all of this. A few years ago, I got a gift bag from a church where I was speaking. It was so thoughtfully done. They had printed pictures of my family from my Instagram and included a few of my favorite things like bottles of sparkling water, almond butter packets, and a couple of bananas with green stems. The green stems just made me feel like, "These are my people. They know what's up with choosing a 'just right' banana!" Then in the bottom of the bag was a bottle of body spray. I pulled it out and sprayed the air in front of me and instantly knew it would be added to my list of favorites.

I liked it so much that I spritzed it on myself several times before heading out to speak.

For months I used this new body spray as my perfume and wasn't shy about telling people about it. One of the people who not only heard about it from me but was also encouraged to buy it was my friend Lisa C. One morning she was in my bathroom helping me get organized while I was out running an errand. She picked up the now famous spray, took a closer look, and immediately texted me a picture of the bottle. "Lysa, is this the spray you've been raving about and using every day?!"

I replied, "Yes! Isn't it wonderful . . . (heart eyes, heart eyes, heart eyes)?!"

She replied with several emojis: "(girl with hand over her face, big-eyed shock face, tears streaming from laughter face) Stop using this as your perfume immediately!"

ME: "Why?"

LISA: "It's *Poop Spray!*"

ME: "Hunh?"

LISA: "It's the spray you use to cover up a poop smell in your bathroom!!"

ME: . . . .

I had no words. For months I had been smelling like a bathroom where unmentionable disposals had happened and been sprayed over. I. Can't. Even.

Please accept my sincerest apologies if you were part of my life during that unfortunate season of "perfume" choices. And to the kindest souls who gave me the spray, I can't imagine how awkward that moment was for you when I walked into the green room that night and y'all tried to decide who should tell me I'd misused your gift. And then the even more awkward moment when you had to decide to just let it go after I went on and on about the new spray you'd given to me. Sometimes ya' girl is a few fries short of a Happy Meal!

As silly as this story is, I see something in myself in this incident that I need to pay attention to. Sometimes good things become wrong things if used in wrong ways.

Poop spray that aids in covering up bathroom smells is a good thing.

Poop spray that is misused as perfume, not so much.

I imagine you already know this. And now so do I. We are already in tune with using many things in the right measure, in the right way, and at the right time. We know there are limits, and we are good with respecting those limits and setting boundaries to ensure we don't pay the consequences for misuse or abuse.

For example, we understand that when a gas tank gets close to empty, we can't just keep driving and ignore the fact that we need gas, or we will eventually get stranded. So, even if we don't feel like stopping for gas, we do. Also, we understand that we must use the right liquid to fill the gas tank. We know we can't just pour water into the tank and hope for the best. We use gas the right way and at the right time.

We understand that when we go to the gym, there are different weights for different levels of strength. We don't have unlimited weightlifting abilities, so we are wise to acknowledge that and work out accordingly. If we attempt to lift weight that is beyond our capacity, we will get injured.

We understand it wouldn't be wise to put a sign in our front yard announcing that the spare key is under the front door mat. Many people are trustworthy, but some are not. Many people have good intentions, but some do not. We know those realities, so we take appropriate safety precautions or risk getting robbed or harmed.

And, as mentioned earlier, we understand that it's not wise to publicly post all our passwords to our bank account, social media accounts, or even movie streaming accounts. We have an understanding that keeping those passwords private is wise or we risk others taking liberties that could frustrate or embarrass us at best and devastate or bankrupt us at worst.

You have put these kinds of boundaries in place because they're wise, not because you are mean, rude, uncaring, unchristian, self- ish, or insensitive. You are a responsible person. You want to be a good steward of what's been entrusted to you. Therefore, you walk in reality instead of wishful thinking. You acknowledge and respect the concept of limitations because you don't like how you act and react when you get stretched too thin. And you wisely establish boundaries when people keep pushing for you to go past your capacity. When people aren't respectful of our limits, we can set boundaries, or we can pay consequences.

You are already doing some boundaries really well.

So why is it we understand boundaries with our bank accounts so much better than with our emotional well-being?

I think it's because we don't truly understand that we have emotional limitations. Just like our accounts can get overdrawn, so can our emotions. Just like spending that gets out of control can bankrupt a person's finances, expending too much emotionally can bankrupt a person's well-being.

We think we can just keep taking it. Overlooking it. Navigating around it. Making excuses for it. Reframing it. Numbing out so we don't have to deal with it. Praying about it. Fussing about it. Crying

> # When people aren't respectful of our limits, we can set boundaries, or we can pay consequences.

about it. Ignoring it. Blaming it. Shaming it. And dropping a million hints about it.

Whatever the "it" is and whoever it involves, please know there is an enormous cost that you and I are probably not factoring in—the trauma[1] it's doing to us. When we allow our emotions to be misused and abused, there will be consequences.

Sometimes we might not even connect the consequences to the stressful situation we are in, like when we experience headaches or unexplainable stomach issues.

> [In one study] researchers followed more than 5,000 participants in Germany for two years and found that the greater the stress in a person's life, the more intense and frequent their headaches were. "Increasing stress resulted in increasing headache frequency for all headache subtypes," said study leader Dr. Sara Schramm, of the University of Duisburg-Essen in Germany. "[Study] participants with migraines experienced more stress than participants with tension-type headaches." Conversely, participants who reported little stress in their lives had few, if any, headaches.[2]

I've suffered consequences in pretty massive ways. What started out as a bad feeling about choices my then-husband was making grew into me having panic attacks. Fear of never quite knowing the truth grew into not wanting to get out of bed some days. A gnawing sense of dread grew until I was constantly bracing myself for another worst-case scenario coming true. Though I tried to process the pain I was in, more and more deceptions were revealed.

And probably the most damaging of all, he was telling me that we were on a track toward healing together, but I was discerning and experiencing a frighteningly different reality.

Internally, I was holding so much confusion, shock, and heartbreak that the physical ramifications were great. Though I'd been a very healthy person, I wound up in the ICU—fighting for my life when my colon twisted so severely that I had to have most of it removed. Then the next year I was diagnosed with breast cancer, resulting in a double mastectomy and a couple of years of reconstruction surgeries. After a long period of hard work with counselors and other professionals, I thought there had been enough healing that an honest and lasting reconciliation was possible. And that was true—until the deceptions and addictions returned. The devastation this time hit me doubly hard as I realized the facts that I could no longer ignore meant the death of a marriage. Within a month of that, my abdominal wall completely separated, a literal hole formed in my midsection, and I was back in surgery all over again.

During this long battle trying to save my marriage, several of my doctors asked me about my level of emotional stress. The doctor who did my colon surgery said my insides were so out of place that it looked like I'd been hit by a bus. When I assured him that I had not been in an accident of any kind, he noted that trauma was evident and should not be left unaddressed.

What happened to me during the last seven years of my marriage wasn't just difficult. It almost killed me. I believe there was a definite connection between the emotional trauma and the resulting physical consequences. Please know, I'm not saying we are all going to suffer life-threatening illnesses if a relationship gets challenging. But I am encouraging you to pay attention to how devastating emotional situations can hurt more than just your feelings.

When you are suffering because of choices that affect you but you have no control over, it's time to start naming what's really going on. It's either a situation of misuse of someone's access to you or a situation of abuse of their influence over you. And often it's both at the same time.

One example of a misuse of someone's access is bringing things into your environment that make you feel uncomfortable, unsafe, or threatened. It could be drinking, smoking, offensive language, listening to or watching inappropriate music or movies. It could be gossiping, judging, or being overly aggressive about someone's political, social, and religious views or conspiracy theories. This isn't a complete list, but if these things erode your sense of emotional well-being, it must be addressed.

Some other examples of abuse of someone's access are doing things to you that are disorienting, damaging, demeaning, degrading, or flat-out dangerous. Consider the following questions:

- When you tell others about your relationship do you find yourself exaggerating the small "good things" and suppressing the hard/bad things?
- Are you experiencing abuse but afraid to call it that? (If the answer is yes, seek help immediately from a trained professional.)
- Do you ever discern the other person is lying to you but when you ask them questions they get defensive and angry? Do they then, in turn, make you feel like the crazy one?
- When you see a call or a text from them, do you fear they are about to hijack your peace and send you spiraling emotionally?
- Are you in love with their potential instead of who they are right now?
- In conflict with this person, do you often have to take responsibility for everything while they resist taking responsibility for anything?
- Do you question your worth or your sanity after you have spent time with this person?

- Are you constantly walking on eggshells because you're afraid that one bad decision on your part will make the other person walk away? Or worse, you fear they will forever hold that one thing against you and use that instance as a justification to do whatever, or say whatever, they please?
- Do you feel unable to share exciting successes in your life with this person for fear of them not celebrating you, or worse, attacking or belittling you?
- Do you spend more time trying to save the relationship than enjoying the relationship?
- Do you fear their choices?
- Are they resistant to changing a behavior even though they know it is hurting you?
- Are you suffering more than they are because of what they do?
- What do the wise people in your life, who love you, are invested in your life, and have a good track record of giving helpful advice, have to say about this relationship?
- Are you willing to listen to those people, or do you provide excuses about why they are wrong?
- Are you proud to be with this person? And even more, are they respectful and proud to be with you?
- Does the level of love you experience from this person seem to rise and fall based on what you do and don't do for them?

None of these questions are meant to shame or place blame on another person. But they will help us recognize and possibly name some potential areas of concern.

To bottom line it for you, I want to share a quote from Gary Thomas. In his book *When to Walk Away,* he says, "If someone is getting in the way of you becoming the person God created you to be or frustrating the work God has called you to do, for you that person is toxic."[3]

When we talk about unhealthy relationships and difficult people, there is quite a range of what this can mean. There's a difference between difficult relationships that have issues that need to be worked through and destructive relationships that are causing harm to the individuals and others around them.

If you have given someone access to your emotions and they are irresponsible and don't consider how their actions are affecting you, pay attention. You'll know it by the amount of anxiety that stirs up when they are around. The person who continues to break your heart isn't in a place to properly care for your heart.

Our bodies are created to react to alarming situations. It's hardwired in us. There is a part of the brain called the limbic system that helps us override the analytical part of our brains and kicks us into fight, flight, or freeze mode. When people lived in the days of sabertoothed tigers it would have been detrimental for someone to get too analytical about what to do while the tiger was baring its teeth and clawing its way closer and closer to them. Instead, their body got an extra dose of energy to react so they could get the heck outta there.

Today, most of us aren't dealing with unusually large tigers chasing us. But we are dealing with the jolt of energy that comes when we are alarmed by misuse and abuse. That energy is anxiety. And that anxiety is compelling us to do something about whoever's actions are making us feel that something isn't right.

Anxiety has gotten such a bad rap for way too long. We are told not to be anxious (Philippians 4:6). That is biblical and good. But remember, the focus of this verse and the surrounding verses isn't to shame us for being anxious but rather to remind us that the Lord is near and what to do proactively with our thoughts when anxiety comes.

Rejoice in the Lord always. I will say it again: Rejoice! Let your gentleness be evident to all. The Lord is near. Do not be anxious about anything, but in every situation, by prayer and petition,

The person who continues

to break your heart isn't

in a place to properly

care for your heart.

— upo

with thanksgiving, present your requests to God. And the peace of God, which transcends all understanding, will guard your hearts and your minds in Christ Jesus.

Finally, brothers and sisters, whatever is true, whatever is noble, whatever is right, whatever is pure, whatever is lovely, whatever is admirable—if anything is excellent or praiseworthy—think about such things. Whatever you have learned or received or heard from me or seen in me—put it into practice. And the God of peace will be with you. (Philippians 4:4–9)

Now, here's something interesting: if you keep reading past these verses to Philippians 4:10 and 4:14, Paul says he rejoiced greatly that his friends were "concerned" for him and that it was good that they "share in [his] troubles." So, when I put all of this together, it seems Paul is not saying that we shouldn't be concerned or that we shouldn't acknowledge our troubles. And I especially appreciate that he doesn't tell us to be silent about our troubles. We sometimes need others to help us process and navigate the hardships we are facing.

But what Paul is teaching us in Philippians 4:4–9 is what to do when anxiety gets triggered in us.

The feeling of anxiety is like an alarm bell alerting us to remember the Lord is near, so we don't have to overreact; we can let the peace of God protect our hearts and minds, and intentionally direct and filter our thoughts, factoring in what is still good. And keep putting into practice these good principles.

It's understandable that you and I feel anxious when someone is misusing or abusing the access we give them. But we need to let that anxiety be an alarm and not a constant state of being.

For example, if you have a small business and you start noticing that your company credit card has some mysterious charges without corresponding receipts, you will probably want to implement more accountability for the employees using the card. Or you will want to stop letting them use the company card until a better checks and balances system can be implemented. The concern over the mysterious charges served as an alarm letting you know a change was needed. If you don't implement the necessary boundary with the card, your anxiety could turn into animosity and make you suspicious of all your employees and possibly even foster distrust with everyone.

Or maybe you have a best friend you love dearly but she has exhibited a pattern of saying she'll do something and then never follows through on it. Up until now, it's been with smaller things that felt too insignificant to address. But the more it happens, the more you start to feel you can't really count on her and you're hesitant to commit to doing things with her. Then, she asks if she can throw a baby shower at your house for another mutual friend. You want to say yes, but you fear you'll wind up carrying the weight of the entire gathering. Based on past experiences, she'll drop major details, show up late, and not have half the food that the two of you agreed she would bring. You know you don't have the emotional capacity to deal with all that could probably play out with this shower, so you make the wise choice to say no. You are still willing to contribute in some way, but hosting it at your house would require a level of responsibility from your friend that she hasn't previously shown when you've given her that kind of access. When your friend asks why you can't host the shower, you don't have to overexplain or even have a big, sit-down conversation about boundaries. You can simply state that you don't have the capacity right now, thank her for understanding, and offer to help in other ways that don't hyperextend you.

Or there's been an issue in your marriage, and you want to have an open, healthy conversation with your spouse. But based on previous conversations that have gone poorly, you tend to personalize what he says, and he tends to bring in past grievances, causing everything to escalate and get off topic.

So, you decide in order to continue to keep this level of access to each other's tender concerns, ground rules need to be established so you each know how to be responsible and caring toward the other. You might say, "In order for us to stay in this conversation, we need to agree not to attack each other, raise our voices, get defensive, or bring up other grievances or topics that aren't related to the discussion at hand. If any of these occur, we will have to pause the conversation and try again at another set time. For both our sakes, I am unwilling to move forward in a conversation that turns hurtful."

Like I said before, the person causing us anxiety in our relationship must start being more responsible or we must reduce their access. If someone is unwilling or unable to stop misusing the personal access we've given them, then we must change their access to match their level of responsibility.

But how?

Here are five factors to help you set good boundaries:

1. A BOUNDARY ISN'T TO TAKE CONTROL OF THE OTHER PERSON'S ACTIONS

The purpose of a boundary is to help you stay self-controlled and safe. A friend of mine recently said, "I thought I was setting a boundary, but I was actually just trying to control the situation by forcing the other person to change." If your focus is trying to change the other person, you will quickly feel like boundaries don't work for you. It's time to shift your focus to what you can control with your boundary:

- Your environment
- What you are, and are not, willing to tolerate
- What you do, and do not, have to give

Your boundary should help set the stage so your emotions can stay more regulated, you can regain a sense of safety, and you can feel more empowered to make necessary changes.

2. GRACE HAS A PLACE IN
THIS CONVERSATION

We can be gracious in how we talk about our concerns, our need for a boundary, and the consequences if the boundary is violated. My counselor, Jim, always says, "Say what you mean, mean what you say, and don't say it mean." Remember, a boundary will most likely mean a change in this relationship for you and for them. It's not wrong for them to ask questions and maybe even want to know a timeframe for how long this boundary will last. We can be gracious in how we inform the other person and answer any questions that are reasonable and appropriate. Another helpful statement Jim taught me when having a potentially challenging conversation is: "Get curious, not furious." You may find it helpful to ask questions about their concerns instead of making assumptions and accusations. Again, we don't want to overexplain or debate our need for this boundary. But we can be gracious in our communication around this boundary.

Pre-decide and possibly even script out what you will say. We will look at some scripts together, but as a rule of thumb, I try to start with empathy and acknowledge something positive about the other person before addressing what must change.

There are many Bible verses that could be helpful here but two of my favorites I repeat to my frustrated self so often that I have them memorized. Proverbs 15:1 says, "A gentle answer turns away wrath, but a harsh word stirs up anger." And Colossians 4:6 says, "Let your conversation be always full of grace, seasoned with salt, so that you may know how to answer everyone." This doesn't mean we don't say the hard things or set boundaries. It means we recognize we want conflict resolution instead of conflict escalation.

3. BOUNDARIES HELP YOU FIGHT
FOR THE RELATIONSHIP

Boundaries are for your sake and theirs so you don't have to keep fighting against unhealthy behaviors, attitudes, and patterns. We can set a boundary, or we will set the stage for simmering resentments. Simmering in the frustrations of knowing things need to change, or trying to get the other person to change, is way more damaging than a boundaries conversation. Yes, boundaries can feel risky. But it's a much bigger risk to delay or refuse to have needed conversations.

4. A BOUNDARY WITHOUT A REAL CONSEQUENCE
WILL NEVER BE TAKEN SERIOUSLY

We have to consider the consequences for crossed boundaries with wisdom and logic. A boundary presented as a hopeful wish is nothing but a weak suggestion. And a boundary presented as a threat will only do more damage. If we can't or won't follow through with a consequence, then that person will eventually stop respecting what we have to say and ignore all future boundary attempts. I've found it very helpful to think through consequences ahead of time and process them with my counselor or wise friends. Here are some ways I try to structure my consequences:

- Avoid using the words *always* and *never* or any other language of extremes.

- Remember you are establishing a boundary in support of the relationship, not against it. This isn't an accusation against the other person. You are simply readjusting their access to match the level of responsibility they've demonstrated in the relationship.
- The consequence should be a statement, not a question. You don't need to ask their permission to implement a boundary or the consequences that go along with it.
- The consequence can be discussed but it does not need to be justified or explained. This one is usually hard for me. I tend to want to overexplain and get to the place where they approve of why I need the boundary. So, I sometimes have to speak directly, not harshly, to remind myself, *Lysa, you are informing them, not debating the validity of your need.*

It's often people who need boundaries the most who will respect them the least. Don't be surprised or caught off guard by this. You can return kindness for this frustration and even empathy for their anger. But see this as an affirmation you are doing the right thing. Stand firm and state the consequences with dignity and respect.

5. PLAY OUT HOW THIS BOUNDARY WILL BENEFIT YOU

Sometimes we feel the pain of setting a boundary and that can make us forget the good reasons we're setting boundaries. In number three above we talked about how boundaries are beneficial for both parties in the relationship. So, let's remember that there is also the benefit of what a boundary will do for us personally. We are taking responsibility to keep our own sanity, safety, and serenity in check. We aren't responsible for the other person's choices, but we are responsible for our actions and our reactions.

Remember, you set boundaries to help you stop feeling so stuck and powerless and allow you to get to a healthier place. It's important that you think through the positives of setting boundaries and rehearse stating them clearly beforehand from a place of strength, so if things get tough and emotional you won't give up. It will be challenging if you have to implement the consequences, but if you've already made peace with this whole process, you won't get nearly as confused and frustrated. Getting to a better place is good even if it doesn't feel good in the moment.

We will cover this more in the next chapter, but as we wrap up this chapter, I want to give you some good starters to needed conversations on boundaries:

"I can tell you care a lot about politics and the issues you are passionate about. Thank you for wanting to share all your thoughts with me. But, I'm in a place right now where I need to guard my heart from the intensity that can sometimes arise in these kinds of discussions. Thank you for understanding that if the conversation about certain topics gets too heated, I'll either need to redirect the conversation to less triggering subjects or we will have to hit the pause button."

"I love you and I care about you. And at the same time, there are some behaviors that are requiring me to make changes to our relationship. When you _____ [insert the unacceptable behavior, substance abuse, or addiction] in my presence, it affects me in ways that I am no longer willing to accept. This isn't an accusation or judgment against you. You're an adult and your choices are your own. This is me being proactive about my well-being and making wise choices for myself. So, I am requesting that you no longer use these substances [or insert other unhealthy behavior] around me or in my home. If you are

A boundary without a real consequence will never be taken seriously.

unable to agree to these parameters, then we'll need to limit our interactions and I can no longer have you visit my home. Again, this is because I care not only about my well-being but also about keeping our relationship in a more sustainable place."

"Thank you so much for considering me. While my heart always wants to say yes to opportunities, the reality of my time requires me to say no. Again, I'm honored you thought of me and I hope your _____ [insert the activity they were inviting you to participate in or asking you a favor for] goes incredibly well. Thank you for understanding and, as always, I'm cheering you on."

"I wanted to talk to you today, not to debate your choices but to let you know it is no longer sustainable for me to stay in the same kind of relationship with you. This isn't an accusation against you. I'm just accepting the reality that this issue is affecting me mentally and physically, and it's time to acknowledge that and make some necessary changes. I'm committed to caring well for myself. Therefore, I have decided to stop asking you to change and instead create some distance between us so that simmering resentments don't overtake our relationship. This isn't easy but it is necessary. If you would like to continue working on our relationship, I am willing to do that as long our interactions are only in the presence of my counselor."

"Thank you for being willing to talk about some challenges we've been experiencing in our relationship. Let's keep this conversation calm and kind. If things escalate to yelling, blaming, or hurtful words, I will excuse myself, and we will have to resume it at another time."

These scripts are just a few examples you can tweak to make work for you. And certainly, I acknowledge the entanglements of difficult emotions, past hurt, present trauma, and many other challenging nuances will make these boundary communications more complicated in real life. However, we need to make it a goal to not get pulled into overcommunicating or justifying or explaining ourselves ad nauseum and risk giving up on pursuing healthier relationship dynamics.

Now, before we close, I'll give you one more script to use in case a certain author named Lysa comes into your presence with a certain spray used in a certain unfortunate way.

"I'm so glad you liked our gift. And honestly, I like the smell so much that I read the fine print and discovered the spray is in fact just for the toilet room! I mean, it smells so good, I can totally see wanting to use it as a quick little body spritz, but don't be tempted. Lots of people have it in their toilet rooms, so we don't want your sweet self to have a covered-up-poop scent following you around all day. And by the way, your hair is really looking fabulous these days!"

A note from Jim on the limbic system

Dysregulation is when an external trigger causes you to go into your limbic system (fight, flight, or freeze mode), which is an automatic physical response to a perceived threat.

The limbic system is essential for scenarios when we need to be on high alert, like if our child runs out into the middle of the street. It's obvious that the child's physical safety needs to be prioritized and we know to rescue the child from danger. The anxiety quiets when an appropriate action restores feelings of safety. A problem arises when our limbic system tells us the situation isn't safe, but we don't know what to do.

If you are in a relationship where you're about to have a conversation during which it's likely that your limbic system will get triggered, plan ahead of time how you will respond. We can prepare in times of security so we're strong in times of insecurity. When we feel powerless, we can rely on pre-planned and rehearsed boundaries.

Helpful tips for when you feel triggered:

- You can be honest that you are feeling triggered and it's best to call a time-out. It's wise to avoid trying to continue a conversation when you are flooded with anxiety.
- Move your body.
- Drink water and wait twenty minutes for your prefrontal cortex (the "thinking" brain) to resume logical thoughts.
- If you say something you regret, be gracious with yourself. Don't berate yourself. Say, "I am human. Knowing my story, my response made sense. I offer myself compassion, and I take responsibility for my actions and reactions. And if I need to ask for forgiveness from the one I hurt, I will do so."

Now, Let's Live This . . .

REMEMBER:

- When people aren't respectful of our limits, we can set boundaries, or we can pay consequences.
- The person who continues to break your heart isn't in a place to properly care for your heart.
- If your focus is trying to change the other person, you will quickly feel like boundaries don't work for you.
- "Say what you mean, mean what you say, and don't say it mean." —Jim Cress
- It's often people who need boundaries the most who will respect them the least.
- A boundary without a real consequence will never be taken seriously.

RECEIVE:

A gentle answer turns away wrath,
    but a harsh word stirs up anger. (Proverbs 15:1)

Let your conversation be always full of grace, seasoned
    with salt, so that you may know how to answer
    everyone. (Colossians 4:6)

REFLECT:

- In your own words, why are healthy boundaries such a benefit to your well-being?
- What thoughts come to mind when you read, "Boundaries are for your sake and theirs so you don't have to keep fighting against unhealthy behaviors, attitudes, and patterns"?

PRAYER:

God, sometimes this topic of boundaries is really hard. Even though I know boundaries are necessary, it's easy for my heart to begin to feel overwhelmed. I pray for peace and courage as I press into how this could all take shape in my life. Thank You for showing me more of Yourself through the words I'm reading. I trust You to lead me so I can use more wisdom and have better discernment in all my relationships. In Jesus' name, amen.

Special note: For further help with boundaries around your time and scheduling, see my book *The Best Yes.*

CHAPTER 6

They May Never See Your Boundaries as a Good Thing

It was one of those days when I needed to just sit outside and stare up at the sky. I repeated to myself over and over, "The sky isn't falling. The sky isn't falling. The sky isn't falling." I knew this in the logical part of my brain. But when *my* world was falling apart, it very much felt like *the* world was falling apart.

I wanted to tell the sky it was lying to me. It *was* falling. I just couldn't see it. When you feel it but don't see it, I think that's the purest definition of raw fear.

Anxiety coursing through me. My chest tightening and twisting. The breathing I couldn't slow. That was all the evidence I needed to know, despite what I saw above me: the implosion of a relationship was happening in front of me.

For months leading up to this day, I kept trying to manage my anxiety around clues that things weren't right. I was doing all the things I've been advised to do when I felt the edges of panic starting to close in on me. Thank you, therapy. After several years of working with my counselor I knew the regimen by heart. Drink at least four ounces of water. Pray a simple request for help. Give myself at least twenty minutes for the limbic part of my brain to settle down a bit before trying to make any decisions or have any hard discussions. Go outside and put my feet in the grass and look up to be reminded the world is still spinning. Go for a walk. Listen to music that calms and feeds my soul. Process with a wise, safe friend who can help me see what I might be missing or assure me that I'm not crazy.

All those things help.

But when the bottoms of my feet started having permanent grass stains, it was time to stop trying to manage the anxiety and instead investigate the source.

I wanted things to be alright. I wanted calm.

But calm didn't seem to want me.

Calm is like setting a thermostat at the right temperature for keeping a house cool on a blazing hot summer day. But if there are doors and windows that stay open, letting the heat in, you're still going to feel the effects of the outside heat. The wrong tactic would be to stand at the window, telling the heat that it can no longer come inside your house. The right tactic would be to shut the windows and doors and let the air conditioning unit work to accomplish the atmosphere you want.

I wanted calm, but the dilemma I was in was causing me so much anxiety because I hadn't been willing to acknowledge where the heat was coming from. I didn't want to make a big deal out of something that, in the grand scheme of all the schemes of life, didn't seem like a big deal.

I didn't want to seem like "that girl" who is overly dramatic or petty or not mature enough in her Christianity to just "overlook an offense." But I had overlooked this offense so many times and the situation still wasn't changing. The person involved didn't live in my house or even in the same state, but her words carried so much weight in my life that just a few harsh statements felt like daggers to the most tender places of my heart.

When this person was in a hard situation, she felt it was completely acceptable to fly off the handle emotionally and verbally berate me. Or she would use numbing substances to the point that she either checked out completely or made no sense when I was trying to talk things through. That opened the door to her saying and doing things she wouldn't normally say and do. I couldn't predict what would trigger her. And no matter how I tried to address the issue, we didn't ever make positive progress that stuck.

This person didn't consider how her actions and reactions were affecting our relationship. She refused to acknowledge the impact all this was having on both of us. It's also important to say that I didn't always get things right in our conversations. But I was committed to fostering an environment between us where there was no yelling, we let the other person talk without interrupting, we wouldn't make accusations, and we would have empathy for each other.

This person didn't see any need to embrace healthier ways of communicating. The way things had always been was still so very acceptable to them. But it was so very eroding to me. The doors and windows were open. The heat was coming in, and I just kept begging it not to. As if the heat might just one day rise up, turn from my house, and suddenly acknowledge my passive wish.

The heat coming in isn't just uncomfortable. It can also be damaging. Last summer I looked at houses with my friend Madi. (It's one of my crazy hobbies to help people find starter homes. I get so into it that it's not uncommon for me to wear a headlamp while climbing into the attic, looking underneath the house, or pulling up air vents to see if I can smell anything ominous. I'm like Inspector Gadget except with basically no legitimate skills.) We were so excited when a house with great-looking bones and loads of potential popped up as available. We had to see it. And when we did, the minute we pulled up in front of it, we knew. This was Madi's future house.

We walked inside. It was *full* of potential. But it was also full of this strange, filmy mildew. The air conditioning had not been on for months. The heat and moisture had simply done what heat and moisture do. And it was a bigger deal than what the previous owner who turned off the air conditioner ever thought it would be. It wasn't just the heat. It was what constant heat can do when it goes unaddressed too long.

Understanding that heat is not just uncomfortable but potentially damaging in certain situations helped me to consider something important. Passivity wasn't working. Wishful thinking wasn't working. By not addressing the situation I wasn't being self-controlled. I was avoiding. And possibly even enabling behavior that could no longer go unaddressed.

I kept thinking, *Am I making too big a deal of this? I mean, this isn't a life-altering situation, right?* All the while it was absolutely altering my life. Note the grass stains on my feet.

So, what was going on here?

I had been going to counseling for a couple of years when I started to feel this weird gap not only in this relationship but in some of my other relationships as well. I was trying to move forward in healing. I was learning how to address issues. I was growing. I guess, in some ways, you could say I was learning how to become more emotionally mature. I wasn't doing this all perfectly, but I was committed to consistently becoming healthier.

As I mentioned before, some of the people in my life were on the same journey of growing emotionally and spiritually. But others were not. And as I continued to pursue progress over time, it only exposed the major differences between healthy behaviors and unhealthy ones. It almost started to seem as if some people in my life were more and more offended by my efforts—more and more frustrated with my definition of what was acceptable and was no longer acceptable—and more and more resistant to addressing issues.

Please hear me when I say this. I didn't feel that I was better than the people who weren't pursuing emotional growth. I was just desperate enough for help that I finally tended to my issues. And in the process I grew, but others weren't on the same trajectory. And navigating this was becoming more and more painful. They were comfortable in the dysfunction. I no longer was.

My friend Candace recently said to me, "Your healing will bring out the emotional immaturity of those around you not willing to pursue health for themselves."

At first when she said this, I tilted my head and thought, *I don't want to label anyone else emotionally immature. That seems judgmental. That makes me feel like I'm saying I'm better than they are.* I have worked so hard to get to a healthier place and hopefully maturing emotionally. I've spent years now inviting my counselor, close friends, and trusted family members to help me be more aware of unhealthy mindsets, patterns of thinking, and ways of reacting that needed to grow and mature in myself. There was so much I had to learn.

And there were so many setbacks and tears and reverting to old ways of thinking and reacting. Having your life turned upside down is brutally devastating, but it can help shake loose some emotionally unhealthy issues that need tending. So, as I sat with Candace's statement, I decided I needed to process this with grace and truth. When the person I was feeling berated by refused to participate in healthier ways of communicating, I would not use the term "emotional immaturity" as a statement against them but rather as a way to name the uncomfortable tension that had arisen in our relationship, acknowledge the gap, and figure out what to do.

If this is you, don't be surprised by the tension caused by relational strain. And when you decide to establish boundaries and the other person tries to label you as controlling, difficult, or uncooperative, see it as a compliment. Yes, you read that right—see it as a compliment. They are frustrated with you because you are no longer willing to participate in the unhealthy patterns of the past. You have decided to raise your actions and words to higher levels of maturity. And if someone chooses not to join you, there will be great tension. In every relationship there are patterns of relating. If you change the pattern and the other person doesn't agree with the change, there will be agitation.

The tension exists because you are doing the difficult work of no longer cooperating with dysfunction.

Let that last sentence sit with you for a minute.

Reread it. Think about it. Consider where and with whom this is playing out in your relationships.

My counselor, Jim, always reminds me, "What people don't work out, they act out." Their unwillingness to address the issues driving their behavior is their choice. You cannot force people to do what they are not willing to do. You don't need to fight it. Agree with it and accept it. Grieve someone's refusal to keep growing, but don't beg them to see your boundaries as a good thing. They may never see your boundaries as a good thing.

Your light exposes something inside of them they'd rather keep hidden in the darkness. So, of course, it's offensive to them. It's painful to feel exposed. It's only natural for them to lash out, but they are just trying to turn off the light as quickly as possible. It's not a personal attack against you (although it will certainly feel excruciatingly personal at times). It's an attempt by that other

> The tension exists because you are doing the difficult work of no longer cooperating with dysfunction.

person to protect whatever illegitimate ways they are getting their legitimate needs met.

Examples of how this might show up will vary, like gambling instead of holding down a regular job, porn, sex outside of marriage, slandering people who intimidate them, trying to one-up others' achievements to prove how great they are, spending money they don't have, shaming and blaming you, substance abuse, saying mean and cruel things to you or about you, using manipulative tactics to try to stay in control of you, or any other unhealthy choices they make that are negatively impacting your relationship. You have a right to be concerned. Sometimes the problem is that you're more concerned for them than they are concerned for themselves. And chances are you are very aware of how their actions are affecting you while they are either not aware or not concerned. When there's this kind of mismatched affection, here's what you have to know. You will never be able to stay where you are and lift them to a more mature or healthy place. They have to do the work themselves.

Did you ever do the activity in high school where one person stood on a table and the other person of equal weight sat on the ground and they tried to see who could get who on their level? The person on the table was never able to pull the person on the ground up to their level. Almost every time, though, the person on the table would get yanked down to the floor. This is true with levels of maturity and health as well. The hardship isn't just the tension between where you are and where they are. The real risk is the longer you stay in this tension, the possibility increases that you'll get pulled down. Remember, our motivation is to love people well, and to do this we can't allow ourselves to get into such an emotionally drained and unhealthy place that this isn't possible.

When you attempt to have honest conversations about the issues at hand (not the other person's emotional immaturity) with loving care as the motivation, and you are rejected or attacked in return, the relationship will need to change. The mature person has a choice to sink down or rise above and stand firm in their health. Obviously, this will cause more and more distance in the relationship the greater the chasm widens between two people who are in different places emotionally.

As I've said before, health cannot bond with unhealth. A refusal to grow and mature emotionally is a big indication of unhealth.

The American Psychological Association defines emotional maturity as "a high and appropriate level of emotional control and expression."[1] Emotional immaturity, on the other hand, is "a tendency to express emotions without restraint or disproportionately to the situation."[2] Pay close attention to the words *without restraint.* When someone demonstrates a consistent inability to exercise restraint in their emotions and actions, they've been stunted at some point in their journey to maturity. If you've ever seen an adult just about lose their mind and their character with a grocery store cashier over a $2 coupon, chances are they have reverted to an age between four and fourteen. We can all revert to the age we were when a childhood trauma happened and remains unhealed. That's why we have to work through these things and grow into a maturity enabling us to use restraint.

Mature people can disagree but still respect the sanity of the other person. Mature people are willing to see the impact their actions are having on the other person and make reasonable adjustments. Or, if they are unwilling to adjust, mature people at least communicate their unwillingness and acknowledge that the relationship may need to change significantly. They do all of this without accusing, abusing, or losing it.

It's immaturity that creates the crazy-making effect of causing you to doubt reality, second guess what is true, and get yourself so off-kilter you stop addressing what obviously needs to be talked about.

Another person's immaturity will always be felt by a mature person. You may not be able to put your finger on it, but you will ask, "What's going on here?" The person may be extremely intelligent and successful and even quote Bible verses left and right but lack emotional maturity.

That doesn't mean we should leverage this in judgmental or demeaning ways against them. Remember, but for the grace of God, we could be doing some of the same things they are. We don't want to grow hard, angry, or develop an attitude of superiority when setting boundaries. We must stay humble and surrendered to Jesus in this process. So, let them have their own journey and revelation. Be wise with setting and keeping your boundaries and remember that you don't have to stay in the same place the other person is in. And use these insights to help you become more aware of what's at play, so you don't keep feeling like the crazy one and discounting your discernment.

If I were you at this point, I would be tempted to say, "Now wait a minute, Lysa. The person does act emotionally immature sometimes. But other times we have great conversations and real connection. It's just hard and confusing when I sometimes see glimpses of such good potential."

Sister, what you see in glimpses should be what you see the majority of the time. If the glimpses of kindness and potential are what's keeping you going, then eventually you'll start accepting even harsh things as good. If you find yourself so grateful for the smallest common courtesy, you're hanging your hope on nothing but air. If your friends think you are accepting too little and at the same time you're wondering if you're expecting too much, pay attention to that. And if you're too afraid to talk about any of this with your wise friends, that's not just a red flag—it's a full-on fire.

If you feel you have to trade the best of who you are to protect the worst of who they are, do not ignore this red flag. Consider the following list to help you identify where you might be in a dysfunctional dance with someone who is exemplifying emotional immaturity:

- They resist needed conversations or turn them against you. For example, when you bring up a topic that needs to be addressed, their denial of the issues at hand and the surrounding facts leaves you feeling like the crazy one.
- They go back to unhealthy coping mechanisms when they have a bad day or a hard conversation.
- They lack self-awareness or are emotionally tone-deaf—they are unable to understand how people perceive them.
- They have an out-of-proportion reaction to a conversation or the situation at hand.
- They don't recognize the inappropriateness of their facial expressions, tone of voice, or timing in bringing up certain things.
- They tend not to own any of their parts of a conflict, always saying, "but you . . ." in response.
- More times than not, they lack empathy in situations and do not consider how their choices will affect the other person.
- They are unwilling to honor or respect any communicated boundaries.
- They do not take responsibility for themselves or their actions and expect you to pick up the pieces.
- They refuse to acknowledge how unhealed trauma from their past, possibly even their childhood, needs to be worked out so it's not acted out.

- They rewrite history to prove a point that serves only them or their version of the truth.
- Their version of reality is not consistent with facts.
- Their version of the truth is what protects them, and they really can't discern what is and is not deception.
- They let their emotions get the best of them and sabotage what otherwise should have been a beautiful moment.
- Instead of acknowledging or confessing wrongdoing, they sweep it under the rug and hope they're not caught.

You may read this list and think parts of it describe you. I understand. Parts of this list describe me too. But at least we're self-aware enough to acknowledge what we still need to work on! If we're progressing toward emotional maturity, we're not staying stuck in immaturity. We'll discuss this further in the next chapter, but for now, there's one more thing to note.

Emotionally mature people aren't eager to weaponize the list above against other people. So, let's continue to examine ourselves and see what we need to see. Acknowledge what we need to acknowledge. Be aware of what we need to be aware of inside ourselves and in our relationships with others.

If you find yourself thinking through some relationships where evidence of emotional immaturity is present, I get it. We don't need to fear this. And we don't need to keep staring at the sky, waiting for a piece of it to finally fall. We need to lift up our eyes . . . from where our help comes (Psalm 121:1–2).

As I processed more on a personal level, I started to wonder, *What does the Bible have to say about emotional maturity?*

It's important that I let truth guide me and quite honestly boss me around a bit. Because here is what I know I'm in danger of: My personality leans in the direction of being more passive than aggressive. I want things to just resolve on their own and get better over time. Then there is the pressure I feel as a Christian woman to turn the other cheek, be gracious at all times, and do everything I can to smooth things over. But if I'm honest, overly passive reactions haven't been serving me or others very well. While being passive may look good at first, if I'm letting the tension of the situation build and intensify, I run the risk of getting so worn out from the hard dynamics at play that I start slipping back into immature reactions and unhealthy patterns.

One of the things that surprised me while I was studying Scripture is the connection between emotions and sobriety. Most of the time we simply think of sobriety as saying no to substances that make us lose control. But having a sober mind can also be an instruction not to let ourselves get out of control with our emotions as well. Let's look at 1 Peter 5:8 (ESV): *"Be sober-minded; be watchful."*

This verse is giving us two responses that are important to keep in mind. First being "sober-minded" and second being "watchful." The NIV uses the word *alert*. What is Peter addressing here? It's anxiety. In verse 7 (ESV) Peter instructs us to cast "all your anxieties on him, because he cares for you." And then in the second half of verse 8, after "Be sober-minded; be watchful," the verse continues, "Your adversary the devil prowls around like a roaring lion, seeking someone to devour" (ESV). Peter is telling us what to do with our anxiety. We are to cast it on the Lord. And we are to be alert and sober-minded. God has a part, and we have a part.

Peter reminds us that while it is true that God wants us to give Him our anxiety, we also have a responsibility to stay clear-headed and pay attention to what is affecting and triggering our emotions. Here's what I don't see in this passage about dealing with anxiety: *passivity.*

We aren't just encouraged to take action—we are commanded to be actively sober-minded and alert.[3] In fact, as I studied this further with my counselor, who has a strong theological background, he pointed out that emotional maturity can also be seen as emotional sobriety in connection with this verse.

There is an intentionality required in being sober-minded. The word *sober-minded* in Greek is νήφω (nēphō), which means to be "self-possessed, clear-headed, and attentive to what is going on."[4] One Greek lexicon (dictionary) says this word means "to curb the controlling influence of inordinate emotions or desires (and therefore become reasonable); conceived of as sobering up from the influence of alcohol."[5] This means to be sober-minded has to do with maintaining control over ourselves. Just like when someone drinks too much alcohol, they have to "sober up" to regain control, to be sober-minded means regaining control over our actions and reactions. Remember, we have an enemy who doesn't just want to tempt us—he wants to devour us. He wants us to act and react out of control. And he wants our thoughts to spin out of control.

The word *watchful* in Greek is γρηγορέω (grēgoreō) and means to be alert, awake, watchful.[6] In other words, it means to not be asleep, distracted, numbed out, or anything else that would stop us from being alert and aware. In biblical times, this was the expectation of the watchman who sat in the watchtower overlooking the area all around a walled city. He was to stay vigilant and pay keen attention to any possible danger. The greatest threat for the watchman may have been the moment he started to nod off, got distracted, or stopped being aware, which meant he was no longer alert.

Both words *sober* and *watchful* warn of losing control. Peter reminds us how important it is for us to play an active role in our lives as we fight against the enemy and his various tactics to lure us into a loss of self-control.

So how does this relate to a need for boundaries with someone displaying emotional immaturity or a lack of emotional sobriety? In the next chapter, I'm going to walk you through a few practical ways that you can establish and communicate healthy boundaries with less-than-healthy people.

But for now, I want you to get a glass of water and set it on a flat surface in front of you. See how the water level on the left side is equal to the water level on the right side? Water seeks its own level. In other words, when you look at a glass of water sitting on a flat surface, the surface of the water is consistently flat across the top from the left side to the right. Never have you seen a glass of water sitting on a flat surface where the water is low on one side and high on the other. Just like gravitational forces help the water achieve equilibrium, so will the pressures of life make it evident if there is equilibrium in a relationship or not. Healthy equilibrium in a relationship is possible only when both people are equally committed to these things:

- healthy habits
- self-awareness
- empathy for the feelings of the other person

When one person dabbles in unhealthy habits, refuses to look at themselves through the lens of reality, or stops considering the feelings of the other, there will be an ever-increasing tension until you sink to where they are or they rise to where you are. Only you can decide how to either manage that tension or say "enough is enough" and make changes. My hope is that we can make healthy changes instead of letting things get to a point where the only choice we have is to end the relationship. Boundaries aren't easy. But they are better than so many other harsh realities. And they are definitely better than standing in the grass, staring up at the sky, and being utterly convinced pieces of it are about to fall.

Healthy equilibrium in a

relationship is possible only when

both people are equally committed

to these things: healthy habits,

self-awareness, and empathy for

the feelings of the other person.

— yps

A note from Jim on boundaries pushback

What people don't work out, they act out. When someone doesn't work through their issues, they'll make their issues your issues.

When someone has internal chaos from what hasn't been worked out internally, they will often stir up external chaos and point the finger of blame. Blame is an attempt to medicate unhealed pain. So, when you try to establish boundaries to protect yourself from the chaos, they'll see this as an extremely offensive move and will try to manipulate you into feeling guilty, so you drop your boundary. A manipulative person has never met a boundary that they liked! Chances are the manipulator has unhealed trauma or childhood wounds from the past that make them resistant to any perceived control over them.

A manipulative person will see your boundary as a yellow light while you intended it to be a red light—with a full stop—to ensure your safety. A manipulator will intentionally speed through that intersection, risking whatever damage may happen to themselves or to you. A manipulative person will do *anything* to resist feeling controlled.

If a person has unaddressed childhood trauma, when someone draws a boundary with them, the person may revert to an age when they first felt unsafe. The boundary you see as a protection to keep the relationship healthy, they will see as a personal rejection.

Now, Let's Live This . . .

REMEMBER:

- Having your life turned upside down is brutally devastating, but it can help shake loose some emotionally unhealthy issues that need tending.
- The tension exists because you are doing the difficult work of no longer cooperating with dysfunction.
- "What people don't work out, they act out." —Jim Cress
- If you find yourself so grateful for the smallest common courtesy, you're hanging your hope on nothing but air.
- If you feel you have to trade the best of who you are to protect the worst of who they are, do not ignore this red flag.
- Healthy equilibrium in a relationship is possible only when both people are equally committed to these things: healthy habits, self-awareness, and empathy for the feelings of the other person.

RECEIVE:

I lift up my eyes to the mountains—
    where does my help come from?
My help comes from the LORD,
    the Maker of heaven and earth. (Psalm 121:1–2)

Be sober-minded; be watchful. (1 Peter 5:8 ESV)

Be on your guard; stand firm in the faith; be
    courageous; be strong. Do everything in love.
    (1 Corinthians 16:13–14)

REFLECT:

- "Your healing will bring out the emotional immaturity of those around you not willing to pursue health for themselves." How do you relate to this?
- When you read this sentence, "They are frustrated with you because you are no longer willing to participate in the unhealthy patterns of the past," what situations came to mind? What are some of the unhealthy patterns in relationships you are no longer willing to participate in?
- When have you felt like you had to trade the best of who you are to protect the worst of who someone else is?

PRAYER:

Father, this journey to health and wholeness isn't hopeless. Help me stay sober-minded and alert. As I choose to stop participating in unhealthy behaviors and dysfunctional relationship patterns, I am asking for Your help. I know boundaries are not easy but help me make healthy changes. As I draw necessary boundaries, please help me process any disappointment I'm simultaneously feeling. I believe You have good things in store for me. In Jesus' name, amen.

CHAPTER 7

Just Because They Say It Doesn't Mean You Have to Own It

Somewhere along the way, I picked up a mindset that I'm still working really hard to untangle myself from. I'll get to that mindset in a minute. But first, let me share a little bit about the way I process life, which initially made me the perfect candidate to resist boundaries and see them as unkind. I can still remember sitting in an elementary school classroom and learning the golden rule: "Do unto others as you would have them do unto you."

I don't remember if I was in first or second grade, but I do remember that the chalkboard in the classroom was massive and the bulletin board to the right of it was impressive. The bulletin board was colorful and cute with a quote at the top that changed daily and was meant to inspire us to take our education and our character development seriously. Below the quote was a list of class-room rules with the golden rule holding the prominent spot as rule number one! Then below the rules were the names of all the kids in the classroom, pinned in neat rows with three strips of paper under each name. There was a green strip, a yellow one, and a red one. The goal each day was to keep the green paper under your name, which meant you were kind, responsible, and respectful of the teacher and your classmates.

If a student violated those directives, the teacher called him or her to the board to unpin the green card and place the yellow card on top for all the world to see. And then, if a yellow-card student still couldn't stay in line, he or she would have to pin the dreaded red card under their name and was sent to the principal.

I was so fearful of the yellow and red cards. I didn't understand that the rules were to help us learn how to be responsible humans. Those rules evoked in me a great fear of being judged as a bad person.

So, to me, following the rules meant that I would be known as a good person. And I didn't just want to be good so others would accept me. I felt I must be known as a good person in order for me to accept myself. Of course, as a child I didn't have the awareness to verbalize any of that, but I remember with absolute clarity the dread I felt going to school most days.

I felt I had to do everything possible to never ever have a yellow or red card attached to my name. Those cards wrongly became a definition of who I was as a person. But here's where things got very complicated in that little classroom. I saw good kids get on the wrong side of some not-so-good kids. It became their game to make up stuff about the good kids and then convince the teacher to call the targeted student up to the board and flip their card to yellow. Some kids saw this as a funny game and brushed it off. I had a much more severe reaction. This was no game. This was a nightmare.

Now, even if you aren't a rule follower, I still think there's something we can all relate to here. This whole thing wasn't just about following the rules. It was about managing people's perception of me. And I think most of us, no matter what our natural bent is, don't want to be misunderstood, misrepresented, or have intentions assigned to us that are not true.

We don't want wrong narratives assigned to us that misalign with who we really are. If we are strong, we don't want people to get the impression we are weak. If we are compassionate, we don't want others to say we are selfish. If we are responsible, we don't want to be portrayed as careless. If we are hardworking, we don't want to be labeled as lazy. If we are committed to living like Christ, we don't want others to accuse us of characteristics that make it seem we don't take our faith seriously.

So, in my mind, the dynamic in that classroom meant that not only did I need to follow all the rules, but I also had to stay on everyone's good side. I did everything I could to keep the perception my classmates had of me in line with who I wanted to be known as.

It was exhausting—but it seemed inescapable. I wanted to be seen and known as good. After all, to be seen but completely misunderstood produces a weight of judgment that can be brutal on a fragile heart still trying to figure out life. And while wanting to be good might seem like a wonderful quality for a child to have, being desperate for others to validate me was not healthy. It set me up for a mindset that's not good at all.

The mindset I mentioned at the beginning of this chapter is this: people's opinions define who we are.

If we live with this mindset, we will be desperate to try and control people's perception of us. We will spend our lives managing opinions to always be favorable toward us so we can feel good about ourselves.

But think about the tragic reality of that mindset. Being too concerned with gaining the approval of others can give us a divided heart with God. Galatians 1:10 points out this issue: "Am I now trying to win the approval of human beings, or of God? Or am I trying to please people? If I were still trying to please people, I would not be a servant of Christ." Plus, it's impossible to please all the people all the time.

We know this. Until we forget—especially with people whose opinions affect us. So, when we disappoint people, think differently than they do, don't do everything they think we should do, or try to draw boundaries they don't agree with, then others might think poorly of us. And if they think poorly of us, we fear it will be impossible to feel good about ourselves.

CORE FEAR

In all honesty, this isn't just something I struggled with in elementary school. It's something I still wrestle with today. Maybe to varying degrees we all do? I think this hits at the core fear around setting boundaries: If I set a boundary, someone will no longer see me as I want them to see me. They will no longer know me as I want them to know me. They will no longer believe the best about me, and there's something inside of me that really wants them to believe the best about me.

So, when we try to set boundaries and people respond with statements that don't accurately portray who we are, it can feel as if we're being absolutely misunderstood and wrongly labeled. Then to fight against that negative label being put on us, all too often we drop the boundary. We would rather suffer through the other person's boundary violations than deal with them judging us wrongly.

Ugh. Hello, me. Hello, you?

I just faced this recently. I presented some opposing facts at a meeting during which my town was going to vote on a new policy.

The policy didn't pass and as a result the people who wanted it became so frustrated, they accused me of being unreasonable. It absolutely broke my heart. After going to bed that night after the meeting, I actually woke up at 3:00 a.m. feeling so panicked over being misunderstood, I got physically sick to my stomach. I couldn't figure out why I was so torn up over this. I had told the truth. My motives were pure and my reasons for presenting were good. But the accusations of the people on the other side of this issue made me wonder if instead of speaking up I should have just suffered through what their proposal would have done to my own family and community.

I'm still processing those feelings but some good verses I keep clinging to are Colossians 1:10–11: "So that you may live a life worthy of the Lord and please him in every way: bearing fruit in every good work, growing in the knowledge of God, being strengthened with all power according to his glorious might so that you may have great endurance and patience."

I want to keep myself in the place of living a life worthy of the Lord. I want to please Him. I want to bear fruit. I want to grow and be strengthened by God. I want to have endurance and patience. That's what prompts me to ask myself, am I more or less likely to live out these verses without a needed boundary? My answer is that I'm less likely so I must keep the boundary until the Lord tells me otherwise.

Remember, you may be feeling logical right now in the quiet safety of you and me walking through this book. You might be nodding your head thinking, *Yes, I need to set a boundary, and I think I can do it.* Right now, the boundary makes sense. But what if, when trying to apply your boundaries in an emotionally charged moment, you lose your resolve, because the other person makes statements that confuse you, make you question the validity of this boundary, or accuse you in ways that hurt? You need to be prepared to know what to do.

See if you've heard any of these types of statements from others. Assess whether these statements have contributed to you giving up on setting boundaries with certain people.

When they say:

"What I did isn't that big of a deal. You're being so dramatic."

"You are being overly sensitive."

"And you call yourself a Christian?! Jesus wouldn't treat people this way."

"I thought Christians were supposed to be forgiving."

"You've got such a hard heart. Jesus would have never walked away."

"This is just more evidence of you being controlling and unforgiving."

"Jesus loved all people and gave grace no matter what. So, what's your problem?"

"You don't seem like yourself. You've changed."

"I'm so disappointed in you."

"You're just crazy and this is irrational."

"You're so selfish. All you care about is yourself."

"Seriously?! How can you be so mean after all I've done for you?"

"You're so off base. Drawing boundaries isn't biblical."

"But you're my (wife, daughter, best friend, mother, sister). Acting this way toward me is out of order and unacceptable."

Here's why these statements are so triggering:

1. **They are offensive.** They aren't an accurate picture of what's true about who we are. Being misunderstood is so brutal because someone else is taking liberties with our identity.

2. **They are threatening.** When someone makes hurtful accusations and pushes against our boundaries, it can feel as if whatever this relationship is providing for us will be taken away and some need in us will go unmet.

3. **They are disillusioning.** When someone else makes us question our need for the boundary, we can second-guess reality, our sanity, our rationality, and even the severity of what's really going on. We can easily start to wonder if the real problem is *us* rather than considering the source and why we are in this hard dynamic in the first place.

It is so very important that we are aware of all three of these feelings that can make us vulnerable to not establishing wise boundaries. Here's the first thing we need to notice about the effects of these triggering statements: they are each evidence that we need to establish a boundary with this person.

And here's the second thing to notice: if we are afraid that this person will think poorly of us, potentially abandon us, or try to make us feel crazy for taking a step toward making the relationship healthy, chances are even higher that, without wise boundaries, they will eventually do all three of these things to us. (Dear me: read that last sentence one more time . . . maybe ten more times.)

Unhealthy people typically don't manage their emotions and expectations (self-regulate) very well and can easily get offended when their lack of responsibility doesn't become your emergency. Their thought process is often that their need trumps your limitations. And the telltale sign of their unhealthiness is their unwillingness to accept *no* as an answer without trying to make you feel terrible, punished, or unsure about the necessity of the boundary.

If we want to stay healthy, we have to use our limited energy in the right way. We could waste years putting all our efforts into trying to change the other person's mind or prove to them why we need the boundary, or worst of all, we could drop the boundary altogether and continue living in dysfunction.

Let me state something crucial. I don't want us to suddenly start categorizing everyone around us as healthy or not healthy. But we must pay attention to those who accept our healthy boundaries and those who resist them.

The apostle Paul addresses some key components to love: "And this is my prayer: that your love may abound more and more in knowledge and depth of insight, so that you may be able to discern what is best and may be pure and blameless for the day of Christ." What I like about Philippians 1:9–10 is that the love here is associated with knowledge and discernment. So, the inverse is also true. A lack of wisdom and discernment is actually unloving. Sometimes we only associate love as a feeling. But we have to remember that biblical love is an intentional action where we want what's best for us and the other person. Keeping this in mind, when setting boundaries our heart posture should be one of wisdom and discernment for the sake of true and healthy love.

Healthy people who desire healthy relationships don't have an issue with other people's healthy boundaries. Hebrews 5:14 reminds us that mature people "have trained themselves to distinguish good from evil." That word *distinguish* means someone can discern more readily what is the right way to treat someone and what is not acceptable. What someone should say and what someone probably shouldn't say. And just because a person *can* do something, doesn't mean she should *do* that thing. Discerning and choosing one's actions carefully leads to a wisdom that those around them can trust.

Healthy people are mature people. They seek to

- understand your concerns,
- discuss any issues that the need for the boundary reveals, and
- respect your limits.

> Healthy people who desire healthy relationships don't have an issue with other people's healthy boundaries.

Remember, healthy people who desire healthy relationships know how to be responsible with the access you give them. For example, if they borrow your car, chances are they won't return it on empty. But if they do, you can let them know that if they want to borrow it again, they just need to replace the gas they use. And they should see that as a reasonable request without making you feel anything less than generous.

Even if someone doesn't like a boundary you have set, healthy people know the difference between hurt and harm. A friend who constantly runs late may feel hurt that you are no longer willing to ride with her to events but can recognize your boundary wasn't put in place to cause her any harm. She won't think that you're selfish and rude. Nor will she blame her issues on you. And she certainly won't diminish your identity, disrupt your safety, or disregard your assessment of reality. She'll either adjust her untimeliness and ride with you or just meet you at the event. Either way, she will respect you enough to respect your boundaries.

Healthy people understand your limits because they are in touch with their own limitations. They communicate what they can and cannot do—what they are and are not willing to tolerate. And they expect you to do the same.

Understanding this can help us realize sometimes the problem isn't that we aren't good at setting healthy boundaries. Maybe we aren't good at recognizing that we won't get healthy results from unhealthy relationships.

CHECKING OURSELVES

Somewhere in all the looking around at others for validation, we've stopped looking up. If we are living honest lives that honor God, we must not forget that people not liking our boundary does not mean we aren't living right before God.

When someone says something that hurts or offends us when we draw a boundary, it can be good to check ourselves. Is any part of this an attempt on our part to do harm, control, retaliate, check out, or give ourselves permission to be irresponsible? While checking ourselves is healthy, questioning our identity is not.

Checking ourselves means looking at a current attitude or behavior to see if it is in line with God's instructions and wisdom. Questioning our identity is doubting who we are because we have given too much power to other people by letting their opinions define us.

I don't know any other way to say this except to be absolutely direct: If our identity, the foundational belief we hold of who we are, is tied to an opinion someone has of us, we need to reassess. We must be honest with how much access to our heart we've given to this person. It's not bad to give someone access to our heart but when we give an unhealthy person too much access, it can shake us to our core. When their opinion of us starts to affect how we see ourselves, we can lose sight of the best parts of who we are because we get entangled in the exhausting pursuit of trying to keep that relationship intact no matter the cost. And when this is the cycle we are caught in, sometimes we would rather manage people's perceptions of us than care for ourselves and the relationship by putting appropriate boundaries in place.

Remember, we talked about personal access and responsibility in previous chapters. When we give people personal access to us, those people must be responsible with it. And emotional access to our hearts is especially important.

We won't get healthy

results from unhealthy

relationships.

— UPS

It's no wonder we are anxious and feel boundaries are only acceptable and legitimate if the other person agrees with and respects them. In other words, instead of stating our boundaries and ending the sentence with a period, we tag on a question. "You good with that?" "Okay?" "Does that work?" "This is understandable, right?" "You see where I'm coming from, yes?" Posing a boundary as a question opens us up to be questioned, debated, and disrespected. If a boundary is presented with doubt, it won't be effectively carried out.

Now, add on top of that the weird notion that if we are Christians, then we are absolutely obligated to sacrifice what's best for us in the name of laying down our lives for others. (You can turn to page 217 for some specific scriptures that have been wrongly used to make people feel guilty about their boundaries.) Where did we get the idea that we aren't allowed to say *no*, have limitations, or be unwilling to tolerate other people's bad behavior? If we are filtering our thoughts of boundaries through wrong perceptions, it's no wonder many of us find boundaries not just challenging but pretty close to impossible.

Here's why:

We aren't sure who we really are.
We aren't sure what we really need.
We aren't sure that if others walked away from us, we'd
     be okay.

We'll get to what we need in the next chapter, but for now let's take an honest look at an important question.

Who are you?

When I took time to answer this question for myself, I wondered why I'd never addressed this before. In a moment of honest

> Posing a boundary as a question opens us up to be questioned, debated, and disrespected. If a boundary is presented with doubt, it won't be effectively carried out.

reflection, it felt incredibly freeing to state for myself who I really am rather than when I'm trying to defend myself against the judgments of others.

Here's who I am. I am a woman who loves God and loves other people. Therefore, because of Christ in me (Galatians 2:20), I am empowered to be the version of me God intended when He created me. I'm kind, creative, caring, generous, fun, and loyal.

I have those qualities, but they aren't what is most apparent when people use me, take advantage of me, make unrealistic demands of me, and make wrong assumptions about me when I say no. In other words, when I've let someone violate my boundaries, I can get so frustrated that I act in completely opposite ways from the woman I really am. This type of reaction is on me—and I need to totally own it—not what someone else does, but my reaction to what they do.

So, boundaries help me stay true to who I really am. Without boundaries, I can hyperextend myself to the point where I become anxious, bitter, resentful, angry, annoyed, and distant. That's not who I really am, so it's my responsibility not to let another person's actions and expectations wear me down to the worst version of myself. In a biblical sense, it's me not allowing another person to make me betray who I am in Christ.

Okay, *your* turn to answer this crucial question: *Who am I?*

Pause here. Think about this.

And if you're having a hard time answering, maybe it's because you've lost her. Sometimes we've let other people's opinions and needs define us for so long that we lose ourselves in the process. Or maybe circumstances have been so confusing, maybe even brutal, that we feel like life has reduced us to someone who others feel badly for. I've felt this exact way during the past several years of my life. I wanted to be a victorious woman of God, not a victim of a bunch of circumstances that caught me off guard and ripped the rug out from beneath me.

There is so much more to us than just being a sum total of what's happened to us. Right?! So, how do we get back to that person we were before all the hard stuff?

I was on a group Zoom call recently with my friend Amanda after she had read an early version of what I've written here. She got choked up as she told me about a picture her mom found in her grandmother's jewelry box after she passed away. The old black-and-white photograph was of a beautiful little chubby-cheeked baby with dark hair.

"That little face in my grandmother's jewelry box was one I hadn't seen in more than twenty-five years since I last laid eyes on the picture. Twenty-five years. It's me as a baby. The most pure version of me. This is me before life happened and wrote its own story on me. Before I got hurt and heartbroken and jaded and run over by what life had become."

Her tears spilled down her cheeks as the rest of us tried to manage the lumps in our own throats. The baby in the picture was Amanda, but the truth of this moment applied to all of us.

Picture yourself as a tiny baby fresh from God's hands. Innocent. Blissfully unaware of tragedy and trauma. Imagine yourself looking into her eyes. What would you say to her? Who do you want to tell her she is before life gets written on her? Speak that over her now.

Remember, you are closest to who you really are when you are the closest to who He created you to be.

Another memory you could recall is to remember yourself before you were really hurt. Before she said what she said. Or he did what he did. Or, before that event when everything changed, and you felt a bit damaged. Who were you?

Think of a memory, a memory from early on in your life, and try to remember who you were before you started looking to others for validation. Before you started becoming so hyperaware of your faults and frailties that you stopped seeing yourself as worthy, valuable, and designed by God on purpose. If nothing comes to mind from your early childhood, just speak to one of your baby pictures and tenderly tell her why she doesn't need to live her life with an unhealthy pursuit of constantly seeking validation from people.

Now, write down the qualities that are true about the most authentic, wonderful version of you.

That's your beauty. The goal is to humbly, and purposefully, walk in that beauty and own it. Serve from that fullness. Give from that wholeness. Walk confidently in the fact that our all-sufficient God did not make you insufficient or broken. Yes, we need to grow and develop and seek to become more and more like Jesus. But just like a seed contains everything in it necessary to bloom, so do we. All that a seed goes through to grow into a plant is part of the process of becoming what it was designed to be—not a process of determining its worth or value (1 Corinthians 15:38–44).

This exercise is more important than you know. If we don't know who we are, we will constantly be manipulated into who others want us to be or become enmeshed in the needs of other people.

When we know who we are, we are whole and available to love, serve, and give to others from that fullness. If we don't know who we are, then we will love, serve, and give, hoping people will fill our empty places and make us feel whole. And in doing so, we will always be defined by how well or how poorly someone else makes us feel.

Now, that's just the introduction to this chapter. My passion for all of this may have put a tad too much wind in my sail—or words in my chapter. Welcome to my overextended TED talk. Just kidding. We are really coming to the end.

In the next chapter, we'll build on what we've learned here. There's an even more secure foundation to knowing who we are than just naming it for ourselves. We want to let God's Word become the words of truth for our identity. When God is the source of our identity, we are much less prone to others feeding our insecurity.

But before we turn to the next page, I want to do something different right here. Together, we've processed a lot in this chapter. Sometimes we need to read. Other times we need to sit with what we've read. Now is the time for sitting and pondering. Take a deep breath. Take a bubble bath. Or play some praise music.

Or if you think better when you move your body, go for a walk. Or a run. (That ain't gonna be me because I don't want to hack up a lung while trying to tend well to my heart. But to each her own.) Take a minute to dance it out to your favorite song. And if it's not a praise song, sing it to Jesus like it is. Or, my favorite, ride your bike while belting out your favorite song like it's a personal soundtrack of your life right now. The point isn't what you do. The point is to reflect and remember who you are.

As you let all these words sit with you, pray and ask God to help you receive from Him who you really are. He created you and made you in His very own image. Capture an image of His goodness and you'll find some part of you there.

I'll leave you with these words I first wrote in my journal and then put in my book *Uninvited* years ago: "God's love isn't based on me. It's simply placed on me. And it's the place from which I should live . . . loved."[1]

A note from Jim on talking to your younger self

If you could go back to a younger version of you, maybe even at a time when you made some mistakes, what would you say to yourself? Would you speak words of contempt or compassion? Compassion says, "Here's how I would protect you now. Here's how I would help you. Here's how I could provide you a safer environment." Based on that example, what words of compassion would you speak over your younger self? Often those are the same words of affirmation you need to speak over yourself now.

Now, Let's Live This . . .

REMEMBER:

- Healthy people who desire healthy relationships don't have an issue with boundaries.
- If our identity, the foundational belief we hold of who we are, is tied to an opinion someone has of us, we need to reassess.
- Posing a boundary as a question opens us up to be questioned, debated, and disrespected. If presented with doubt, a boundary won't be effectively carried out.
- It's my responsibility not to let another person's actions and expectations wear me down to the worst version of myself.
- We won't get healthy results from unhealthy relationships.
- When God is the source of our identity, we are much less prone to others feeding our insecurity.

RECEIVE:

Am I now trying to win the approval of human beings, or of God? Or am I trying to please people? If I were still trying to please people, I would not be a servant of Christ. (Galatians 1:10)

But solid food is for the mature, who by constant use have trained themselves to distinguish good from evil. (Hebrews 5:14)

And this is my prayer: that your love may abound more and more in knowledge and depth of insight, so that you may be able to discern what is best and may be pure and blameless for the day of Christ. (Philippians 1:9–10)

REFLECT:

- Write out your thoughts about the following statement and how this caution applies to your life right now: "We won't get healthy results from unhealthy relationships."
- What do you think it means to be in touch with your own limitations? Why is this important for the health of your relationships?

PRAYER:

Jesus, thank You for being such a safe place for me to return to when I'm struggling with my identity. When I'm tempted to look to others for validation and acceptance, please remind me to look up at You. As I reflect on the truths I've read, I pray that the Holy Spirit would give me eyes to take inventory of my own life, the understandable limitations of my capacity, and personally consider any potential changes I need to implement. Thank You for the grace and patience You have toward me as I grow and learn on this journey. In Jesus' name, amen.

CHAPTER 8

Trying to Make Someone Else Happy Shouldn't Be Your Definition of Healthy

"Mom, we think you need a puppy."

Before my grown kids, who no longer live at home, got to the second syllable of the word *puppy*, I said no. There were many reasons. But mostly I felt like this whole conversation was code for "they wanted all the fun of a puppy without the daily responsibilities of said puppy." If they could talk me into it, they could love him and enjoy him when they wanted, but then choose to leave him with me to do everything else.

So, of course I wound up getting a puppy.

And it absolutely worked out exactly like I thought it would.

But what I hadn't counted on was completely falling in love with this little apricot-colored fur ball of pure joy. And you know how it's wise for some dogs to be crate trained? Yes, well, that wasn't working for my little pup named Givey. Every time I put him in his crate, he cried and cried until I couldn't take it any longer and let him out.

But this pattern wasn't helping in the potty-training department or the don't-chew-up-my-stuff mandate at all.

One day, my friend Shae came over to work on some projects and Givey was in rare form. Everything a good puppy should do he was doing the opposite. After picking up almost an entire roll of chewed up toilet paper strewn across the living room floor, I said, "I know I should put him in his crate for some time-out, but I just can't stand to hear him cry."

Shae replied, "You know, my mom had a really wise statement she would often say when we were crate training our dog, Rosie. When she started crying and we all felt bad for Rosie, my mom would say, *Well, I'm not happy 100 percent of the time in my life either. She'll be just fine.*"

I mean, Mama Tate has a real good point there.

And just so you know, Givey eventually not only got used to spending appropriate amounts of time in his crate but wound up liking it so much that now he sometimes crawls in it on his own. I think the crate has become his safe place in this big world.

And it certainly brought a lot of relief to my puppy-mom life.

Putting Givey in his crate when I left the house or he just needed some time-out helped establish a boundary between his personal space and mine. If he wants to chew something of his in his crate, great. But in the rest of my home, chewing up my stuff isn't acceptable.

Givey isn't a bad puppy. Actually he's quite amazing. But at the time, he was an untrained puppy. And I think not having boundaries fed his anxiety. He was forced to try and figure out what he could and could not do. This didn't give him a feeling of freedom—it imprisoned him in uncertainty.

Defining what is and is not acceptable is even more important with human relationships. If people are constantly annoying us, frustrating us, exhausting us, or running all over us, chances are we either don't have the right kind of people in our life or we don't have the right kind of boundaries. Or maybe it's both.

Good boundaries bring relief to the grief of letting other people's opinions, issues, desires, and agendas run our life.

But if we see boundaries as a one-way ticket to acting unkind, unchristian, or uncaring, there will be no relief because we will be consumed with the grief of others not being pleased with us. Or we will carry the awful weight of guilt of saying no and fretting over consequences that aren't ours to carry.

Wait . . . relief? You might think to yourself, *Boundaries don't bring relief. They can make the other person angry or disappointed enough in me to say hurtful things about me. I just want to keep the peace, so I'll go along with their attitudes and behavior so that I don't have to deal with the fallout of addressing all of this.*

And friend, that might appear to work for a while.

But make no mistake: over time, you'll have the equivalent of a living room full of shredded toilet paper and a heart full of simmering resentments. Without stopping the cycle by establishing appropriate boundaries, either there will be an eventual emotional explosion of frustration, which you'll later regret, or simmering resentments that will silently eat away inside of you until you truly can't stand that person at all.

Sometimes the worst kind of anger and bitterness happens when you feel forced to smile on the outside while you are screaming on the inside.

I've been that woman. Sometimes losing my temper because

If people are constantly annoying us, frustrating us, exhausting us, or running all over us, chances are we either don't have the right kind of people in our life or we don't have the right kind of boundaries.

I'd let things go so long, I just couldn't hold back my frustration any longer. Or, sometimes biting my tongue so long that I lost the desire to stay close to that person.

I'm not proud of either of these extremes. And neither of these reactions match who I really am as a person. Truly, that's what hurts so much as I look back at reactions I regret. I allowed things to get to such a bad place, I couldn't hold on to the real me.

And when I lost the real me, I never gained anything good back. Losing my temper never made anything better. And stuffing my frustrations never made the hard stuff go away. I knew I needed boundaries, so why was I letting other people's commentary rattle my identity?

In the last chapter we already worked on answering the question "Who am I?" But how do we apply all of this in the context of a really challenging relationship dynamic?

There are countless married women who have reached out to me brokenhearted and feeling paralyzed because of their husbands' struggle with pornography and refusal to get help. Often the wife tries to draw a boundary by saying she can no longer allow this issue to go unaddressed. She declares that she will be going to a counselor to help her process the trauma this is causing to her heart. If her husband would like to join her and work on a healthy solution, then together they can move toward healing.

Good boundaries bring

relief to the grief of letting

other people's opinions,

issues, desires, and

agendas run our life.

— Lysa

If her husband refuses, she tells him that in order to pursue healing for herself, she will make some needed changes. Then she works with her counselor on the necessary boundaries and consequences to keep her heart protected and to keep her from feeling devastated by her husband's actions. She knows boundaries aren't meant to change her husband, force him to see things the way she does, or even teach him lessons. Of course, she wants her husband to stop watching porn. But he has to make that change for himself. So, her boundaries are to help her manage the hurt without constantly losing her temper or getting filled with bitter resentment.

But here's where all of this could fall apart. The wife draws necessary boundaries and her husband lashes back: "It's no wonder I watch porn. Look at what a nag you are. You are so dramatic. This isn't that big of a deal. All men do this. I can't even trust you with my struggles because you're always looking to find something wrong with me. And you think this little boundary tactic is going to make me more attracted to you? No, this just shows me I'm justified because you don't care about my needs."

She's brokenhearted over everything he says. She loves her husband. She's afraid of losing him. She feels so alone. She doesn't feel like she can tell anyone. Now, not only does she have the hurt of his betrayal, but she starts to question if *she* really is to blame. She wonders, *Am I trustworthy? Am I overdramatic? Am I so overbearing that I'm the one pushing him to do this?*

So, she drops the boundary, trying to prove to him that she's none of those things he accused her of and hoping things will get better. But she doesn't realize that in dropping the boundary, the real issue of her husband watching porn goes unaddressed. She is the only one bearing the consequences of his choices and the cycle of hurt from his actions will most likely continue. She will end up devastated, angry, and feeling like a hostage in a situation that never gets better.

After years of unresolved anger, she starts reacting in ways she never thought she would. She makes passive aggressive comments. She gets frantic about knowing where her husband is and what he's doing at all times. She feels so afraid of what he might be doing with his computer and his phone, she tries to control his every move. In essence, she runs the risk of becoming the very thing that she was trying to prove she isn't.

This woman is kind, loyal, responsible, and generous. The only fighting chance she has of keeping the best of who she is front and center in her daily life is by remembering that boundaries aren't shoving him away—they are helping hold herself together. At the core of what's tearing apart her marriage isn't her need for a boundary but rather his inappropriate and unbiblical choices (Galatians 5:19–21).

If you're reading this and are in a similar situation in which another person's behavior is deeply impacting you, I understand.

I relate to the excruciating angst of what deceptions and all kinds of heartbreak do to a wife who wants nothing more than to be fully chosen, purely loved, and honorably protected in the marriage relationship. This is where she allows herself to be the most open and vulnerable, so this is where she experiences the deepest hurt. I have sat with many women who have experienced betrayal. I've wept with you. I've felt bewildered with you. I've cried out to God with you asking for the madness to stop. I've wondered with you why this happens. I've processed with you how we can forgive and move forward. And I've wept with you some more.

And certainly, there are husbands who know this same heartbreak and betrayal as well. When one spouse starts keeping secrets from the other to cover up and continue in hurtful patterns instead of loving their spouse and family, they give the best of themselves to invest in inappropriate relationships. This is some of the deepest pain a human soul will ever know. And it's doubly crushing when addressing those things with your spouse, you're told a narrative filled with half-truths, covered-up truths, or promises to change that they don't intend to keep.

I've carried hundreds of these conversations inside of my head, trying to make sense of actions that won't ever make sense.

It's a brutal journey learning that we can be okay even when the choices of someone we love are not okay at all. Trying to stay whole in the process no matter how fractured this other person becomes, feels like something that sounds good in theory but isn't an option for brokenhearted gals like us.

Watching another person tear apart a life you love hits us in waves of grief. And it's this grief over what we fear we will lose that makes us feel scared to draw boundaries and use our voice to say, "No more!"

We feel deeply, so we hurt immensely. Our mind and pulse are constantly racing from triggers and fears and worst-case scenarios. And though we aren't normally wired for retaliation, sometimes it just feels good to get down in the mud and sling it back on the one hurting us so much.

That's when we must say, this person has already devastated us. And we will not allow this situation to draw us into making choices to retaliate that add the weight of our own regrets on top of all the other pain.

So, how do we keep ourselves together day after day, when someone seems to be working overtime to tear us apart? Again, this is why we must draw boundaries, get help from others, and use our voice to say, "_____ is not acceptable, and I will work to keep myself safe and healthy no matter what my spouse chooses from now on."

Certainly drawing boundaries in a marriage where infidelity and other traumatic issues are happening apply to some of us but not all of us. Regardless, we all must not just draw appropriate boundaries but also guard our true identity.

There will often be everyday scenarios that might make us question who we are based on another person's actions or reactions. For example:

- A close friend not inviting you to be a bridesmaid in her wedding, and suddenly you are questioning whether she really viewed you as a friend.
- Messing something up at work, and your boss telling you that you must pay closer attention to detail. Suddenly you question if you really have what it takes to handle your job.
- A neighbor constantly complaining that you aren't in compliance with the Home Owners Association standards, and you question why you can't ever seem to get it together.
- A parent expressing their disappointment in you for deciding not to travel to their house several hours away for Thanksgiving this year, and you question if this means you really are a terrible daughter.

If you personalize an incident by attaching it to your identity, you'll bear the weight of it like an unremovable scarlet letter. If you don't personalize it, but rather see the situation as a moment to pause and consider, you'll be better able to humbly determine what to do, and how to process it.

Maybe this is an opportunity to ask yourself, is this something that is supposed to reform me or inform me? If some part of this situation helps develop you in healthy ways, receive it as a growth opportunity.

Or if a person's actions aren't helpful but instead hurtful or their requests unrealistic, let this inform your response. Discern . . . do I need to talk to them about this? Do I need to establish healthier expectations? Do we need to agree to disagree? Do I need a boundary here?

Let's take that last example about Thanksgiving travel and apply some wisdom to it.

Consider if this is a potential opportunity to be reformed: Is your parent disappointed because you really have neglected the relationship? Are you not going to see them out of retaliation or unkindness? Did you commit to go, and then another opportunity arose that seemed more fun? Maybe your mom or dad being upset is legitimate and you reconsider your decision.

If not, then consider how this might inform you: Your parent's disappointment may be a sign they are having a hard time with traditions shifting, and maybe you just need to invite them to come to your house. You aren't rejecting them, and you are being realistic about your own family's desire to not spend so much time on the highway. You aren't being unkind. You are being wise about recognizing your own family's need to be together at your home and establish your own new traditions.

Or maybe your parent's disappointment is informing you of some deeper issues and unhealthy tendencies that need to be addressed and setting boundaries would help.

Regardless, here's what we shouldn't do: attach their disappointment to our identity. Someone else being disappointed doesn't make *us* a disappointment. We can listen to the statements of others for the purpose of considering if there's any truth in them and if so, what we may need to receive in humility. But we can't hold onto someone else's disappointment as an indictment of who we are. Remember the example of Jesus found in 1 Peter 2:23: "When they hurled their insults at him, he did not retaliate; when he suffered, he made no threats. Instead, he entrusted himself to him who judges justly."

I don't have all the answers. Not for the everyday relational hardships and hurdles. Not for the woman whose husband is refusing to acknowledge porn as a serious problem that's tearing apart his wife and his marriage. Not for all the other kinds of devastations many have endured. Not for why any of this happens and when it will ever stop. Some of this is all just horribly crappy and uber complicated.

But here's one answer I do have: Other people don't get the final say about who we are. God does. Therefore, what makes it possible to not fall apart into a fractured and frail shadow version of the woman we are meant to be is this: we must place a boundary around our identity, protecting it and guarding it, using God's truth to inform and stabilize what we know, what we feel, and what we do.

STAYING WHOLE

We can't control what others believe. We can't control what others feel. We can't control what others do. But we can control and be responsible for ourselves. As we've discussed before, boundaries aren't meant to control another person. Boundaries make it possible for us to hold ourselves together.

In the last chapter, we discussed the basics of the question, *Who am I?* We wrote down the God-honoring qualities we know to be true about ourselves and committed to living in line with who we really are. Now, let's ask the question, *What makes a whole person?*

I know this is a big question. But it is worth looking at because being whole has a big impact on not only our health but on the quality of the relationships we are drawn to. Whole people tend to gravitate toward whole people. Fractured people tend to attract other fractured people.

Let's take it a little deeper by breaking down this question into three distinct spiritual realities: *orthodoxy, orthopathy,* and *orthopraxy.* Now don't get intimidated by the fanciness of those big words. These terms are new to me as well. But here's why I am so committed to better understanding these deeper terms: I want to be whole. And because I want to be whole, I must keep other people's comments about me separate from what I believe about myself. Therefore, I must stay whole by keeping what I know, what I feel, and what I do in alignment with God's truth about who I am.

Orthodoxy: What we know. Correct doctrine.

But the wisdom that comes from heaven is first of all pure; then peace-loving, considerate, submissive, full of mercy and good fruit, impartial and sincere. Peacemakers who sow in peace reap a harvest of righteousness. (James 3:17–18)

Set your minds on things above, not on earthly things. (Colossians 3:2)

Orthopathy: What we feel. Correct emotions.

A time to weep and a time to laugh, a time to mourn and a time to dance. (Ecclesiastes 3:4)

Bless those who persecute you; bless and do not curse. Rejoice with those who rejoice; mourn with those who mourn. (Romans 12:14–15)

Orthopraxy: What we do. Correct living.

He has shown you, O mortal, what is good. And what does the LORD require of you? To act justly and to love mercy and to walk humbly with your God. (Micah 6:8)

Do not merely listen to the word, and so deceive your-selves. Do what it says. (James 1:22)

I must stay whole by keeping what I know, what I feel, and what I do in alignment with God's truth about who I am.

When all three of these are in alignment with who God intends me to be, that's wholeness. A fractured human being is one who has disconnected some part of their thinking or feeling or doing from who they are.

For example, if I am a kind person, then my thoughts (orthodoxy), feelings (orthopathy), and actions (orthopraxy) should line up with that reality of wholeness. But if I allow the statements and actions of other people to get me so rattled that I start having harsh thoughts, bitter feelings, and snarky reactions, this is a fracture that's probably indicating a boundary is necessary to help me find alignment and wholeness.

If I am a responsible person but I say yes to too many things because I am too afraid of saying no to others, then chances are high that I'll drop some balls. It's not because I'm irresponsible. It's because what I knew I should do and what felt right (saying no to too many requests) got fractured from what I actually did (saying yes to everything).

Just like a fractured arm becomes too weak to be used properly, if we are fractured in our thinking, we won't use our thoughts in healthy ways. If we are fractured in our feelings, we won't use our emotions in healthy ways. If we are fractured in our doing, we won't act and react in healthy ways.

So, what does this have to do with boundaries?

1. Boundaries remind us of the right definition of healthy.

If you are living in the constant tension that the only way to save a relationship is to keep that other person happy, the goal of someone else being happy shouldn't be your definition of healthy. You are whole and healthy when who you are as a child of God is in alignment with what you know (orthodoxy), what you feel (orthopathy), and what you do (orthopraxy).

Our boundaries won't please some people. Our boundaries won't be applauded or appreciated or help us keep everyone happy. Our boundaries won't be the quick fix to make all our relationships feel better. Our boundaries won't be the "hack" to teach people a lesson their mamas never did. Our boundaries won't make us look like the super-Christians able to leap tall buildings and take on the weight of everyone else's issues, irresponsibility, and irrational demands with a smile on our faces.

But what boundaries will do for those of us terrified of being misunderstood is to finally abolish the notion that having limitations and needs is selfish. And we can finally accept that not everyone will be happy with us—and that's not a bad thing at all.

2. Boundaries protect us from fractured people fracturing us.

I want to love the right people well. I don't want to get so emptied by the fractured people that I don't have anything left to give to anyone else. And I don't want to become so fractured myself that I stop functioning as a conduit of God's goodness in this world.

For almost a decade now, relentless hardships and heartbreaks have threatened to shape me and remake me into someone I am not. That's why I've learned to pay close attention to my thoughts, my feelings, and my actions. I hold them up to truth just like Paul teaches us in 2 Corinthians 10:5: "We destroy arguments and every lofty opinion raised against the knowledge of God, and take every thought captive to obey Christ" (ESV).

I'm motivated by that verse, but sometimes I tilt my head and wonder, *How will this truth help me right now in this situation . . . in this heartbreak . . . in this maddening relationship reality?*

Basically, I can't let other people's fractured *thinking* affect me to the point where I get my thinking out of alignment with God's truth. I can't let other people's fractured *feelings* affect me to the point where my feelings get out of alignment with God's truth. And I can't let other people's *actions* affect me to the point where my actions get out of alignment with God's truth.

Because when any part of me gets out of alignment with God's truth, I betray the best of who I am.

We've got to know who we are, so we don't lose ourselves in the fractured realities of others. We can't live our lives to satisfy the unrealistic demands of other people.

So, again, *who are you?* If you are kind, the right boundaries are meant to help you stay kind. If you are responsible, the right boundaries help you stay responsible. If you are loyal, the right boundaries help you stay loyal. If you are generous, the right boundaries help you stay generous. Keep going with this, using the qualities that God Himself would speak over you. Not based on other people's opinions but on who He created you to be.

The question *who are you?* is such an important one. That's why we've taken two chapters to explore this. And if you're recognizing (like me) that parts of your true self have been fractured by being in relationships with fractured people, let's close this chapter by looking at some qualities we can focus on developing. And not just developing, but also living so we can stand confidently with Jesus, the one who secures our identity, so we aren't constantly trying to figure it out for ourselves. Let's open up God's Word and look at Colossians 3.

Colossians 3:12–16 says,

> Therefore, as God's chosen people, holy and dearly loved, clothe
> yourselves with compassion, kindness, humility, gentleness and

patience. Bear with each other and forgive one another if any of you has a grievance against someone. Forgive as the Lord forgave you. And over all these virtues put on love, which binds them all together in perfect unity.

Let the peace of Christ rule in your hearts, since as members of one body you were called to peace. And be thankful. Let the message of Christ dwell among you richly as you teach and admonish one another with all wisdom through psalms, hymns, and songs from the Spirit, singing to God with gratitude in your hearts.

Earlier in chapter 3, Paul tells us to "put on the new self" (verse 10). Paul's language of "put on" would have recalled royal clothing that kings and important kingdom officials would have worn as they returned victorious from battle in biblical times. In a similar way, if a king or an official was defeated in battle, there would be a ceremony where they would take off their royal clothes and put on clothes that represented their defeat as they were usually led to their death.[1]

In Colossians 3 Paul's language of "putting on" and "putting off" speaks to this ancient context. If you and I say we have an allegiance to Jesus but then put on clothes of defeat, which are things like anger, rage, malice, slander, filthy language, and lying, this actually points to a false allegiance.[2]

Instead, Paul tells us to put on our victory clothes given to us by Jesus (compassion, kindness, humility, gentleness, patience, forgiveness, love, unity, peace, thankfulness, wisdom, gratitude). These qualities give the world evidence of our faithful allegiance to our victorious King Jesus.

We are walking in victory. Therefore, we should be wearing our victory clothes. It's not just that we are kind because we have a natural bent toward wanting to be kind. Or that we are patient because we have a natural bent toward being patient. We show these outward qualities because of an inward understanding of who we are. The Bible clearly states we are chosen, holy, and dearly loved by God—see the beginning of Colossians 3:12.

The best of who we are is made possible by the best of what God has done for us. He has chosen us. He has set us apart for His holy purpose. And He loves us with an intentional and dedicated love that won't quit on us.

The boundaries we put in place are safeguards that keep our allegiance to Him intact. So, when you answer this question—*who am I?*—Colossians 3 is a great place to start. And please note, these qualities mentioned by Paul are not an exclusive list. Throughout the Bible you can find many other God-honoring qualities to help you put a stake in the ground and declare your allegiance to Jesus—not the ever-changing opinions of others.

Remember the story I told you in the last chapter about the classroom? Recently, I mentally walked back into that room from all those years ago. I made my way up to the bulletin board and focused on my name specifically. I removed the red card. And then the yellow. And I even removed the green one too.

I placed them aside.

I looked at the golden rule and wondered why it now seems I understood it to mean, "Do unto others so they will think well of you." That's not at all what it said. I guess I missed that the golden rule itself is a nod to boundaries. "Do unto others . . . as you would . . . have them do unto you."

In other words, maybe we shouldn't forget to also have others do unto us as we would do unto them.

Then I took the most important step of all. I removed my name from the board and walked out of the classroom. It was time to reclaim who I am. I am who God says I am. And, while I can still appreciate and love the well-meaning lesson of that board from years ago, it feels so good to no longer be defined by it.

A note from Jim on enforcing boundaries

In this chapter, Lysa gave the example of the woman who was trying to set boundaries after discovering her husband's ongoing issues with pornography. I want to point out that there is a big difference between *trying* a boundary and *enforcing* a boundary. But the first step before the wife does anything should be to get professional support from a counselor who specializes in partner trauma and betrayal, so she is not alone. It's essential that she feels prepared before talking with her husband about boundaries.

With the women I counsel, we develop a strategy for the necessary boundaries to be communicated and implemented in the right timing and in the right setting. We also determine appropriate consequences for specific boundary violations. We literally make a list that says, "If he does this, you do this." What is communicated in vagueness, stays in vagueness, so we want to get as specific as possible.

Here's what the wife really needs to look for: How does her husband respond when she communicates the boundaries? Does he push back and resist the boundaries or is he willing to pursue recovery? Sometimes the worst part of this whole deal is the lying, hiding, denying, and projecting his issues onto her. But the hope in this is when he is willing to not just work on the pornography but also work on healing the trauma inside of him. That trauma is usually the real driving force behind this form of acting out.

The number one reason I don't see people enforce boundaries around pornography and infidelity is grief over what they have lost and what they may lose. I encourage women in distress that many others have gotten through this and they will too. Get support. Get a plan that includes boundaries, consequences, and accountability. Develop a protocol for what to do if the boundaries and plan are violated. If your husband won't go to counseling with you, get individual counseling so you can tend to the personal trauma you're experiencing.

Now, Let's Live This . . .

REMEMBER:

- If people are constantly annoying us, frustrating us, exhausting us, or running all over us, chances are we either don't have the right kind of people in our life or we don't have the right kind of boundaries.
- Good boundaries bring relief to the grief of letting other people's opinions, issues, desires, and agendas run our life.
- Someone else being disappointed doesn't make *us* a disappointment.
- I must stay whole by keeping what I know, what I feel, and what I do in alignment with God's truth about who I am.
- I don't want to get so emptied by the fractured people that I don't have anything left to give to anyone else.
- Whole people tend to gravitate toward whole people. Fractured people tend to attract other fractured people.

RECEIVE:

He has shown you, O mortal, what is good.
    And what does the LORD require of you?
To act justly and to love mercy
    and to walk humbly with your God. (Micah 6:8)

We destroy arguments and every lofty opinion raised
    against the knowledge of God, and take every
    thought captive to obey Christ. (2 Corinthians
    10:5 ESV)

Do not lie to each other, since you have taken off your old self with its practices and have put on the new self, which is being renewed in knowledge in the image of its Creator. (Colossians 3:9–10)

REFLECT:

- Read the following statement from this chapter: "We've got to know who we are, so we don't lose ourselves in the fractured realities of others. We can't live our lives to satisfy the unrealistic demands of other people." How does this speak to you personally?
- What are some of the qualities you like about yourself that you want to make sure the people you love experience when they spend time with you? How can boundaries help make your best qualities more and more apparent?

PRAYER:

Father God, as I think about the truth-filled words I've just read, my heart is comforted by the fact that nothing and no one other than You defines me. Who I am is held completely in the protection of what You have done for me. Help me make choices that stay in line with Your Truth. As I process words spoken to me or over me by others, help me untangle any pieces of un-forgiveness, bitterness, or resentment that I may need to bring to You. Thank You for making a way for me to live the healthiest life I possibly can so that Your light shines even brighter through me for others to see. In Jesus' name, amen.

CHAPTER 9

What Am I So Afraid Of?

I dreaded making a phone call to a person I'd done life and volunteer work with for years. I hadn't drawn a boundary and I knew I should have. Honestly, I'd tried to do boundaries with her many times. So many times, in fact, that I could tell each time I tried again, she didn't take me seriously because I always gave in. Eventually she would always find some way to make me doubt that keeping the boundary was a good idea. I could do boundaries well with other people but not with her.

So, she kept asking for too much. And I kept giving too much.

I'm a pretty high-capacity person. I have a lot of energy, and I truly do love to love and serve my people. And when you can do a lot and it feels good to do so, then it doesn't sound like that big of a deal. Until I hit a limit. All people have limits—physically, financially, relationally, emotionally. No one is limitless. The telling sign that I had hit a limit was the level of anxiety I had when this friend called or texted me. Just the sight of her name on my phone made my pulse race and a feeling of dread wash over me.

So, in the rush of trying to get back to a calm place, I had said yes to a request too quickly and knew I had to call her back and tell her I just couldn't do it. Leading up to this call, I felt an enormous amount of yuck in the pit of my stomach. I want to be a woman of my word, and now I was going to have to go back on what I'd agreed to do. But integrity isn't perfection. Integrity is humble honesty before the Lord and with other people. So, I knew I had to be honest with this friend and approach the whole thing with humility.

I started with an apology. "Please forgive me for originally saying yes to your request when I should have said no. Because I love you, it brings me so much joy to make you happy. And because I want to be at peace with you and be appreciated by you, I let my desire to please you run ahead of my honest assessment of this situation. But now my anxiety about saying yes is sounding the alarm inside my heart that I made the wrong decision. So I need to make a change here and say no."

I wanted her to be understanding. I wanted her to appreciate my honesty and respect how hard it was for me to have this conversation. But there was none of that. Instantly, I could feel her anger. In her mind, me saying no wasn't an option. She wanted what she wanted. And in her defense, me saying yes a few days before had gotten her hopes up, which made this letdown even more frustrating for her now.

But what she was asking of me would have cost me more emotionally and timewise than I had to give. When I initially said yes to what she had asked me to do, I'd put some parameters in place to make this situation manageable. The problem was, there was a long history of her pushing the limits and not respecting my parameters. So, for several days after saying yes, I kept playing out in my mind what could and probably would happen for this whole thing to spin out of control.

Once again, I'd given this person high-level access when I already knew she wouldn't bring that same level of responsibility.

And I put myself in a situation where I was hoping she would make the right choices so my anxiety could stay in check.

I finished the tense conversation by saying, "I should never have put you in a position where I expect you to manage my anxiety for me. That's my responsibility. Therefore, I am willing to disappoint you now to prevent this from turning out poorly for both of us later."

I'd really love to tell you that by the time we hung up everything was all rainbows and heart emojis. Nope. There was nothing fun about it. But there was something so good that came out of it—a moment of absolute clarity for me.

After I hung up the phone, I tried to sort through what was happening in my heart. There was a lot of emotion, but I was having a hard time naming my feelings. Was I proud of myself for communicating this boundary? Was I sad she was so upset with me? Was I disappointed in myself that I couldn't do what my friend was asking me to do? Was I frustrated? Was I relieved?

No, none of those.

The feeling was fear.

I was afraid. But what exactly was I so afraid of?

It was deeper than just being afraid of disappointing her. It was deeper than just being afraid of making her mad and disrupting the peace.

I was afraid that because I told her no and drew a boundary, she would withdraw from me. And she would take something with her that I needed. My motivation in wanting to please her was partly because I loved her, but it was also partly because I loved feeling that if I kept her happy, she wouldn't walk away from me.

That's not fun for me to admit. I'd had a lot of trauma and loss happen in a short period of time. So, the thought of losing one more person panicked me. But becoming a people pleaser wasn't the answer. No trauma is healed in a healthy way by developing unhealthy ways of coping.

I also knew that I shouldn't just pretend I had no needs at all. I once had a friend tell me the best way never to get disappointed by people is to have no expectations of them. But that didn't sit well with me—doing anything to an extreme doesn't feel sustainable to me. Besides, humans were designed by God for community. We are humans with needs, and it should bring us joy to be in relationship with people and meet each other's needs. But here's where I was getting it wrong. I was so afraid of her rejecting me, I kept accepting her irresponsibility as if there was nothing I could do about it.

I wanted to be chosen and valued by her. That's not a bad thing.

But it was more than that for me. Honestly, I felt like *I must be* chosen and valued by her, or I couldn't feel settled and secure.

Did you hear the difference there between "I want to be" and "I must be"?

I want to be is driven by a desire. *I must be* is driven by a demand. And when our desires shift into becoming demands, we run the risk of getting caught in the most serious form of people pleasing. I'm not talking about the kind of people pleasing where we just want to keep someone happy so we can be liked by them. I'm talking about fearing that our needs will go unmet if we draw healthy boundaries with someone, so we let the person take complete advantage of us.

When we are giving most of our energy and efforts each day trying so hard to stay "good" with another person, we stop paying attention to our own well-being. And we run such a risk of becoming the worst version of ourselves: exhausted, depressed, skeptical, distant, insecure, bitter, constantly feeling taken advantage of and manipulated. We can get to such a bad place without even realizing what's happening. And before we know it, no part of what we are doing for people is motivated by authentic love. It's actually not about them at all. It's about us getting from someone what we feel we can't live without.

We can so easily lose our sense of self-worth when we only feel:

- *acceptable* if we are seen as the one everyone else can always count on.
- *in control* when people see us as significant and respect our opinions.
- *valuable* when we have something impressive to give or do for them.
- *loved* when we meet their needs, stay available for what they want to do, and keep saying yes to their requests.

Look at this list below and circle the needs that you often bring into relationships:

To be validated
To be in control
To be liked
To be seen as perfect
To be good
To be in good standing
To be appreciated
To be valued
To be chosen
To be beautiful
To be understood
To be at peace
To be right
To be in charge
To be loved

To be protected
To be unique
To be respected
To be nice
To be supported
To be admired
To be the expert
To be the model Christian
To be the hero
To be the center of
    attention
To be needed
To be accepted
To be the responsible one

Using the needs you circled in this list, do some personal reflection and honest assessment.

REFLECTION STATEMENT

Am I needing to be _____ (example: the hero) *to such an extent that I am unwilling to establish and maintain a healthy boundary? Do I fear that it will cost me too much? It could cost me being _____* (example: admired) *by this person; therefore, the boundary isn't worth it. I would rather things stay as they are than risk a change costing me what people pleasing is giving me.*

Thinking through this is hard for me. And that's the exact point of this whole chapter.

People pleasing isn't just about keeping others happy. It's about getting from them what we think we must have in order to feel okay in the world.

I know some people will say, "I don't struggle with people pleasing."

But if you feel you must have something from others, you might want to keep reading. And if not for yourself then for all the others who may be trying to please you to get what they want.

This type of people pleasing is needing to pursue something from another person for personal gain. But not just to pursue what we think we must have from another person within reason. We can so easily be derailed, distracted, and devastated when we don't get what we think we must have. Therefore, making sure to set ourselves up so someone will meet our needs becomes one of our primary motivations and lifelines to feeling settled and secure. The less we get what we feel we need from someone, the more we are tempted to react in extremes. Either we drain ourselves through all manner of people pleasing, or we eventually give up and walk away.

Good boundaries help us walk in the middle. Boundaries help

us see that it's not wrong for us to have needs. And it's not wrong for other people to have needs. As a matter of fact, it's good for us to clearly state our needs and have honest conversations in our relationships about the realistic needs of both parties. But then it's important to not cross over into demanding that our needs are another person's responsibility. And we must not let other people demand that meeting their needs should be our responsibility.

As I've examined my needs, I've asked myself over and over: Why would I sacrifice my well-being trying to get people to give me what I need at all costs? What am I truly wrestling with? What am I so unsure of? What is the great dread in my soul? Besides just fearing other people will walk away from me, what is the deeper fear driving all of this?

Maybe it's deeper than just my fear of someone rejecting me. While that is certainly part of the reason why I would rather keep saying yes to unrealistic requests from other people even when I know I should say no, there's something even deeper going on here.

Maybe the real core issue is that I fear there will be a devastating gap between what I think I need and what God will actually provide. Maybe I fear I must get from people what I am unsure God will provide for me. And if I fear God's provision is incomplete, I must fill in that gap with other people or I won't make it in this big, sometimes scary, often threatening, and always chaotic world. Therefore, I've made people the answer to my security rather than God Himself.

Yikes.

It's an inverted security that only makes us more and more insecure with every realization that people aren't designed for or capable of filling in the gaps of our doubts about God.

The smoke screen is "I don't want to appear unkind or unchristian in drawing boundaries." But the raw truth is we will always desperately want from other people what we fear we will never get from God.

And for someone else, we can't be what they fear they will never get from God. If we want to be a good spouse, friend, coworker, daughter, sister, or neighbor, it's not by being another person's savior. Keeping someone from feeling their own desperate need for God isn't love—it's cruel. Early church father Origen said, "For he who does not know beforehand of his weakness or his sickness, cannot seek a physician; or at least, after recovering his health, that man will not be grateful to his physician who did not first recognise the dangerous nature of his ailment."[1] If someone doesn't ever become aware of their own need for God, they will never truly embrace what only God can give them.

Trying to please people won't ultimately satisfy us or the other person, and it certainly doesn't please God. I'm discovering that if I have a need and I ask something of someone else, that's okay. But if I have a need and I demand it from someone, that's a sign that I've crossed over into wanting from them what I should be seeking from God. But here's what I've come to understand: God may be allowing that need in me so I will have the motivation to turn to Him.

And the same is true with other people's needs. God may be allowing someone to experience temporary discomfort so she'll turn her deepest longings over to Him and receive what we ultimately can't ever give her. If you are constantly feeling guilty about what your boundaries will cause to happen in another person's life, please reread that last sentence. Of course, allow the Holy Spirit to speak into the nuances of your exact situation and be reasonable and sensible.

We don't want to be void of grace. But we also don't want to rob someone of the good outcome that might happen if they recognize that you aren't an unlimited source. The main point is, we shouldn't and ultimately can't be the one to supply all of what another person needs.

Because God has a limitless supply, only He can meet all our

> We will always desperately want
> from other people what we fear
> we will never get from God.

needs (Philippians 4:19). Because God created us, only He can truly access the depths and fullness of someone's heart (Romans 8:26–27). Because nothing is too hard for God, only He can sustain the type of giving a desperate soul longs for (Jeremiah 32:27).

That is what only God can do for my soul. Your soul. And every person's soul.

Remember, Jesus did do many amazing and sacrificial acts of love for others. He fed people, washed their feet, taught them, comforted them, and modeled a different way to act and think. But He didn't do it so people would fill a need in Him. He served *from* a place of fullness, not *for* a feeling of fullness (Matthew 20:28).

And often He only did for others what they couldn't do for themselves. He offered what only He could do and then required others to do what they could do. Jesus put mud on the blind man's eyes but then told the blind man to go wash in the pool for himself. He didn't run to get the water for him. He healed the lame man and told him to get up, take up his mat, and walk for himself. He didn't carry the man or his mat. Jesus had compassion on the woman caught in adultery. He didn't condone her actions but instead told her to go and leave her life of sin.

Jesus was obedient to God and loved people well. He didn't people please, hoping to be well liked and accepted by everyone. And when people didn't like what He had to say and they walked away from Him, and many people did, He didn't drop His boundary, chase them down, and beg them to take Him back. Jesus loved people enough to give them the choice to walk away.

All throughout Scripture, God always gave His people an option to follow Him or follow their own way of thinking. "But my people did not listen to my voice; Israel would not submit to me. So, I gave them over to their stubborn hearts, to follow their own counsels" (Psalm 81:11–12 ESV).

God calls us to obey Him. God does not call us to obey every wish and whim of other people. God calls us to love other people. God does not call us to demand that they love us back and meet every need we have.

If you are a highlighting person, go ahead and swipe some yellow on those last couple of sentences. Write those on sticky notes and post those truths on your bathroom mirror, on your bedside table, on your phone, your calendar, and even on your forehead if you wish. Okay, maybe not your forehead, but you get my point.

So, what do we do if we are caught in the trap of this type of people-pleasing agenda? It starts with managing our own thought life.

In the situation I mentioned at the start of this chapter, I had to chase down my fear of not getting the security I wanted from my friend and the risk of her walking away from me if I kept a boundary in place.

Let's end this chapter by learning some ways to manage our thoughts. First, let's look again at the Reflection Statement from a few pages ago. I'll fill it out using myself as the example and then you work on your own Reflection Statement below.

Am I needing to be _accepted_ to such an extent that I am unwilling to establish and maintain a healthy boundary? Do I fear that it will cost me too much? It could cost me _being supported_ by this person; therefore, the boundary isn't worth it. I would rather things stay as they are than risk losing what people pleasing is giving me.

Now, let's rewrite it.

I need to be _accepted_. But I now recognize that sacrificing healthy boundaries to get _someone to support me_ is the wrong way to get my needs met.

Now you try it:

Am I needing to be _____ to such an extent that I am unwilling to establish and maintain a healthy boundary? Do I fear that it will cost me too much? It could cost me being _____ by this person; therefore, the boundary isn't worth it. I would rather things stay as they are than risk losing what people pleasing is giving me.
Now, let's rewrite it.

I need to be _____. But I now recognize that sacrificing healthy boundaries to get _____is the wrong way to get my need(s) met.

If we aren't convinced of how much a boundary will help us, we will be too afraid of what the boundary will cost us.

So, if I understand that I am feeling threatened by my fear of what someone will take from me, then before I draw the boundary, I need to weigh the risk and reward ahead of time.

The Risk of Setting This Boundary

I fear that my friend will walk away from me. But if she's the type of person who might walk away now, then even if I try to please her to the highest level humanly possible, chances are she may still walk away no matter what I do.

I fear she will be disappointed in me if I don't do what she wants me to do. But if this is the way this relationship has worked, then chances are she will eventually be disappointed in me anyway.

I fear that I will lose something I don't want to lose if I establish a boundary with this person. But if my friend is prone to withholding her support, then chances are I may lose out regardless.

Healthy relationships don't feel threatening. Loving relationships don't feel cruel. Secure relationships don't feel as if everything could implode if you dared to draw a boundary.

So, in light of all this, what do you fear the most in setting a boundary?

If the fear you just listed above happens, then what?

And what could happen next? And then what? And then? Play this all the way out, step by step.

What parts of your fears are legitimate?

What parts of your fears are being driven by something you feel you must have from this person?

If you don't draw a boundary, what negative effects will this have on you? What negative effects will this have on the relationship?

Think through these negative effects on you. If nothing changes, is this relationship sustainable long term?

By constantly saying yes to this person, how might you be getting in the way of what God might be trying to do with them?

The Reward of Setting This Boundary

To find the rewards, consider some of the following questions. Even if it takes some time to go through these questions, it's worth it. It's better to think through these now rather than suffer through continued relational dysfunctions.

What part of your emotional or physical strength could you get back if you draw this boundary?

What might God do for you if you draw this boundary?

If we aren't convinced of

how much a boundary

will help us, we will be

too afraid of what the

boundary will cost us.

— lys

> Loving relationships don't feel cruel. Secure relationships don't feel as if everything could implode if you dared to draw a boundary.

How might this boundary help you stop feeling powerless or held hostage by this person's opinions, judgments, unrealistic expectations, and unacceptable behaviors?

How would drawing this boundary improve your mood, your attitude, or your health?

How could drawing this boundary help you stop avoiding and start enjoying this person?

How could drawing this boundary help this relationship be healthier over time?

In what ways could this boundary help quiet the fears you've been having in this relationship?

Today I worked on this chapter while sitting near water, watching the sunrise. The water stretched as far as my eye could see and the colors in the sky were mesmerizing. I had a few friends with me, and as we watched the huge, round sun finally crest the horizon, we gasped at the beauty. My friend Shelley said, "Isn't it wild how a ball of fire is close enough to keep us warm but not so close that it burns us up?" It really is the most amazing reality! So I commented, "And isn't it wild that none of us are afraid? I mean, when else would a massive ball of fire appear and everyone just sits and stares at its beauty rather than run away terrified and desperate to escape? But since we know the One who placed the sun there, we aren't afraid. We are comforted and delighted enough to take a hundred pictures."

That's what I want for us and our needs. We know God created us with needs and He placed us in relationships. But, just like the sun, our relationships should be close enough to comfort us but not so close they completely consume us. Lord, may it be so.

A note from Jim on coping

While Jesus does encourage us to be childlike with Him, He does not want us to be childish in how we deal with our adult life. "When I was a child, I talked like a child, I thought like a child, I reasoned like a child. When I became a man, I put the ways of childhood behind me" (1 Corinthians 13:11).

Remember, children have parameters placed on them to make sure they don't use things in excess or harm themselves and others. In times of trauma or relational pain, it's especially important that we pay attention to this and make adult decisions for ourselves as well.

Unhealthy Ways of Coping:

- Binge watching Netflix or TV
- Excessive use of alcohol or drugs
- Rage or retaliation
- Heavy sarcasm or cynicism
- Compulsive spending or emotional eating
- Excessive use of social media
- Use of porn or sexual infidelity

Healthy Ways of Coping:

- Intentional self-care (taking a walk, reading a helpful book, getting adequate sleep)
- Dinner with trusted friends
- Finding a new creative hobby (painting, cooking, writing poetry)
- Participating in regular therapy sessions
- Educating yourself on spiritually and emotionally healthy topics related to your healing (podcasts, Bible studies, online resources, workshops and seminars)
- Journaling and memorizing Scripture

Now, Let's Live This . . .

REMEMBER:

- People pleasing isn't just about keeping others happy. It's about getting from them what we think we must have in order to feel okay in the world.
- We will always desperately want from other people what we fear we will never get from God.
- Jesus served *from* a place of fullness, not *for* a feeling of fullness.
- Jesus loved people enough to give them the choice to walk away.
- When people didn't like what Jesus had to say and they walked away from Him, He didn't drop His boundary, chase them down, and beg them to take Him back.
- Only God is limitless.
- Secure relationships don't feel like everything could implode if you dared to draw a boundary.

RECEIVE:

Just as the Son of Man did not come to be served, but to serve, and to give his life as a ransom for many. (Matthew 20:28)

And my God will meet all your needs according to the riches of his glory in Christ Jesus. (Philippians 4:19)

"Behold, I am the Lord, the God of all flesh: is there anything too hard for me?" (Jeremiah 32:27 ESV)

REFLECT:

- People pleasing isn't just about keeping others happy. It's about getting from them what we think we must have in order to feel okay in this world. Think of a relationship in which you fear telling someone no. In light of what we have discussed in this chapter, what is the real reason you are afraid?
- By constantly saying yes to this person (or these people), how might you be getting in the way of what God might be trying to do with them?
- What could be a benefit to you in drawing this boundary?

PRAYER:

Lord, thank You for always being there for me. You never get tired or weary of me coming to You for help. Please give me discernment as I carefully and prayerfully consider when to extend a "yes" or "no" to others in my life. As I continue to draw necessary boundaries, I ask for Your peace to guard my heart and mind through these difficult decisions and conversations. Today, remind me of how much You love me so I'm less tempted to turn to others for things that I really should be turning to You for. In Jesus' name, amen.

CHAPTER 10

Can a Goodbye Ever Really Be Good?

I have stared my greatest fear in the face. I wish I could tell you that fearing it was worse than facing it, but that's not exactly true. That's like saying bracing for impact before a crash is worse than the actual impact. They are both terrifying. They cause shock. They both can make you hold your breath and scream all at the same time. Experiencing the impact of an emotional devastation has a bone-shattering, heart-ripping, disfiguring effect.

It was the crash that hurt beyond what I ever dared to believe I could bear. The intensity of the pain was more than I could bear. And somehow, I bore it anyway. You and I are alike in this way. Because look at you—you're breathing despite having the wind knocked out of some of your greatest hopes. Dancing with a limp in your spirit. Getting back up and, though you haven't quite been able to completely dust off the rough realities, realizing grit ain't all bad.

You've survived that day. You've survived all the days since. And you are surviving this day too.

So, yeah, you and I are so much more alike than what we'd ever know if we were just passing each other in the bread aisle at the grocery on a random Wednesday morning. We'd both look pretty normal, moving along with the practical details our lives require. And yet somewhere between deciding to go with the whole wheat or skip the bread altogether this week, a memory from the past flashes across your mind and, as you sigh, invisible grief spills out with your exhaled breath.

The memory was a scene from the life that was yours before the loss, the heartbreak, the event that changed everything.

Grief doesn't stay contained. It won't wait for private moments behind closed doors. It will spill out whenever and wherever it hits us. I know this because, just like you, I've experienced it. And the next time you feel intensely alone when you're crying in the bread aisle, remember I'm right there too. There's so much spilled-out grief all over that store.

The movie from my life that popped into my mind while I was in the bread aisle was the briefest memory of the spatula—well past its prime—that we used to flip the French toast we were making for a table full of hungry kids. Back when there was a "we" in the kitchen of our life. Back when it was our table. Our tradition. A shared commonality that isn't shared any longer.

I never knew a simple loaf of bread could trigger such pain. On a Wednesday morning. A midweek, midmorning, mid-aisle, grocery store meltdown wasn't on the schedule. And yet, there it was.

We've survived what we feared. But can we survive the remembering?

Memories are both our greatest treasures and our greatest

sorrows. Great ones are told with heart emojis and exclamation marks and enthusiastic "Remember that time we _____!!" Grief-filled memories are tucked underneath layers of pain written out on emotional scar tissue. And most of the time, when a goodbye has been spoken, memories become an impossible tangle of both grief and greatness, sorrow and celebration, and sighs in the bread aisle on a Wednesday morning.

I wonder why the term is *goodbye*? What's good about a goodbye that takes pieces of your heart you don't want to see taken? What's good about a goodbye that makes you wonder if you'll survive the remembering? What's good about a goodbye that's impossibly permanent, that you didn't want or ever anticipate happening?

We're going to get into the specifics later of how and when to say goodbye. But for now, let's just focus on the foundation of what a goodbye could be.

Honestly, I've really struggled with goodbyes.

I've said before that I'm loyal to a fault. And while that sounds noble it can also be codependent. I'm working on that with my counselor. And I'm working on why I've always felt that to walk away from a relationship is an epic failure for me as a Christian. I wrestled with goodbyes feeling mean-spirited and sometimes they are. But the more counseling I get and the more I study the Bible, I'm starting to gain a different perspective. Maybe the way we say goodbye can help us survive the memories.

Maybe it is possible to end a relationship, being honest about what wasn't healthy, and still celebrate what was good. Maybe it is possible to have real feelings of hurt, betrayal, and disappointment but still see the person from time to time and not want to run into the nearest bathroom stall to text your friend about how much you're freaking out. Maybe it is possible to both be honest about what didn't work and still be good with the memories that were good.

Maybe this isn't possible in some situations. I will absolutely admit that some situations are just brutal and horrific. And to try to treat those situations with a slapped-on, Christianese statement full of Pollyanna pep is inappropriate. Or to try and shame the one who was hurt for being brave enough to say goodbye is beyond cruel. It's stuff like this that can make some Christians seem incredibly out of touch, insensitive, and just plain awful. And I won't tidy any of that up. I'll just say it's wrong. The end.

But what about the other kinds of goodbyes? The ones where there was some good there at one time. There were some beautiful things. There are some good memories even if the good turned bad and an ending was absolutely necessary. Is there a way for us to walk away holding onto our integrity? Is there a way to let someone walk away from us without hating them? Is there any way for a bad goodbye to still be a "good" bye?

It's interesting that the original phrase in the late 1500s was "God Be with Ye." The contraction of that phrase was "Godbwye" which eventually became "goodbye."[1]

I've sat with the thought of goodbyes being more of a sending off with God rather than a slammed door, a contact deleted, and a puddle of angst. Is it possible for a goodbye to be more than a good riddance with a huff of disgust? I wonder, when Jesus watched the rich young ruler walk away, what was the look in His eyes? I wonder, when Peter denied Jesus and abandoned Him just before Jesus went to the cross, what was the goodbye like? A goodbye Jesus surely whispered through a busted-up body and a broken heart? I wonder what it was like when Judas, with a heart full of betrayal, kissed Jesus' cheek, sold Him out, and then wound up hanging himself. How did Jesus say goodbye?

I'll never really know on this side of eternity.

But I have a thought. I think Jesus said goodbye the same way He lived all the days before the hurt, betrayal, rejection, and abandonment. While the relationships certainly changed, He didn't let the goodbye change Him. He let people walk away without letting go of who He was. Even when people turned on Jesus, He didn't let a goodbye turn Him into someone He was never meant to be.

And while I'll be the first one to admit I'm nowhere close to the purity and perfection of Jesus, I also don't want my goodbyes to make it look like I've never spent any time with Jesus at all.

Might it be possible to acknowledge hurt without unleashing hurt?

Might it be possible to admit a necessary ending without unnecessary slander?

Might it be possible to be a little more mature or honoring of God or peaceful about moving on?

I haven't been great about this in the past.

But I'd like to get better.

It's always been my deep conviction to follow where the Bible leads. I don't ever want to start with my opinions and then find verses to try and support my thoughts. I want to start with God's truth and let Him shape my thoughts with His. We don't want to violate God's Word in our efforts to keep God's Word. Clearly in the Bible there are times when we are called to stay, fight, and pursue relationships. However, we also clearly see in Scripture that there are absolutely situations and circumstances when the most God-honoring action is for us to separate ourselves and say goodbye to a relationship.

As I've processed these necessary goodbyes, I'm starting to realize that sometimes, for good to happen, goodbyes have to happen first.

So, I started looking into the Bible to see: Did good people who loved God and wanted to do the right thing ever get to such a hard place with a relationship that they said goodbye?

The answer is surprisingly yes.

Even when people
turned on Jesus, He
didn't let a goodbye turn
Him into someone He
was never meant to be.

— lys

In Genesis chapter 13, Abraham and his nephew Lot decided to separate and live in different locations apart from each other due to the constant quarreling between them and among those managing their flocks and herds. Interestingly, the separation lasted until Abraham rescued Lot and his family from Sodom's impending doom. Though they had lived separately for years, Abraham and Lot eventually reunited when Abraham learned Lot had been captured and needed to be rescued. Abraham sent his men out on a rescue mission and they "brought back his relative Lot and his possessions" (Genesis 14:16).

So, lesson learned: some goodbyes are for a season. But even in those seasons of separation, this doesn't mean you don't care about and watch out for the best interest of the other.

In the New Testament we find that Paul and Barnabas had a "sharp contention" (Acts 15:36–41 NKJV) about taking a cousin of Barnabas named John Mark with them to be a helper for their next missionary journey. When I was looking for more information about this situation between Paul and Barnabas, I found an interesting article:

> They could not reach an agreement, and so they split up. As far as the sacred record indicates, these two remarkable men never saw one another again . . . This dissension between Paul and Barnabas was not over a *doctrinal* issue. The rupture involved a personal dispute based upon a judgment call. To their credit, neither Paul nor Barnabas let the conflict distract them from their respective efforts of spreading the gospel. Making application to Christians today, there will always be times when good brethren will disagree in matters of opinion. The important thing is to keep focused on doing the will of Christ. That is what Paul and Barnabas both did. As a result, perhaps even *more work* was accomplished for the Lord because of the manner in which their disagreement was

Might it be possible to acknowledge hurt without unleashing hurt?

handled. . . . The segmentation of their work did not disrupt permanently the love and respect that Paul and Barnabas entertained for one another. Paul would later affectionately mention Barnabas as being worthy of monetary support in his work of proclaiming the gospel (1 Corinthians 9:6).[2]

So, lesson learned: some goodbyes are not for a season, they are forever. But when two good people part ways and don't cause harm to each other, it may actually allow for more good to be done in their respective callings.

But then what about those goodbyes that are due to blatant sin, toxic behaviors, dysfunctional pride, or destructive actions?

Gary Thomas in his book *When to Walk Away* says,

Some of you still can't imagine turning someone away or letting someone walk away, even if the relationship has become toxic. Your Lord and Savior doesn't have that problem: "Many will say to me on that day, 'Lord, Lord, did we not prophesy in your name and in your name drive out demons and in your name perform many miracles?' Then I will tell them plainly, 'I never knew you. Away from me, you evildoers!'" (Matthew 7:22–23). Jesus actually sends these people away. He spoke the truth and respected people's choices . . . controlling others is a primary sign of toxicity, not a method for ministry. Jesus never cheapened the beauty of what he was saying by appearing desperate. In fact, he pretty much took the opposite approach: *this is what's true; take it or leave it.* That confidence built the early church.[3]

Remember, some people appear to say the right things, but their actions betray their words. Jesus quoted Isaiah 29:13 in reference to such people: "These people honor me with their lips, but their hearts are far from me. They worship me in vain; their teachings are merely human rules." This was in the context of Jesus explaining what defiles a person in Matthew 15. Jesus went on to explain that people like the Pharisees are "blind guides" and instructs those listening to leave them!

> Jesus called the crowd to him and said, "Listen and understand. What goes into someone's mouth does not defile them, but what comes out of their mouth, that is what defiles them."
>
> Then the disciples came to him and asked, "Do you know that the Pharisees were offended when they heard this?"
>
> He replied, "Every plant that my heavenly Father has not planted will be pulled up by the roots. Leave them; they are blind guides. If the blind lead the blind, both will fall into a pit." (verses 10–14)

So, lesson learned: Remember how Jesus defines the blind guide. Matthew 15:19–20, "For out of the heart come evil thoughts—murder, adultery, sexual immorality, theft, false testimony, slander. These are what defile a person." It is not only okay to end a relationship where these things are present, Jesus warns us if we don't, we may run the risk of falling into a pit with them.

I don't want to be a pit dweller. I want to walk in the light. I want to delight in the truth. And I want my heart, mind, and words to reflect my devotion to God. I will not bow down to someone's mistreatment, but I also will not rise up with such angst and anger that I violate God's truth in the way I exit.

I'd like a little more "God be with you" in my goodbyes.

So I've been trying with the goodbye in front of me. Sometimes it feels awkward and awful. Sometimes I'm just in so much pain, I can't muster up any energy to do anything but grit my teeth and blast it all out with my counselor. Some of the memories of what happened will probably always be painful and not good at all. But the thought of "God be with you" has really stuck to something good in my heart. And it's sneaking into my thoughts and my processing and even my conversations.

And then the other night I literally just closed my eyes and pictured Jesus' hands. I mentally started placing all the memories one by one into His strong, carpentry-calloused, nail-pierced, grace-gripped hands. I asked the Lord to help me whisper "God be with you" over each memory. I asked Jesus to help me release some of the memories, hold onto others, and make peace with all that I could. It didn't settle everything yet. But it was a start and I believe that Jesus is working in me and healing my heart. After all, Isaiah 61:1 says that the Messiah would come to heal the brokenhearted. I'm sure I'll also keep unpacking a lot of this in counseling for years to come.

Now I find myself not just surviving the memories but actually thinking I can flip French toast again without crying. And that's good. Good bye. Good bye. God be with you. Goodbye.

A note from Jim on codependence

In the 1970s, the word *codependency* came out of the substance abuse field and described a person struggling with drugs and alcohol. The "codependent" was a loved one or friend of the addict who was trying to help them but ultimately ended up enabling them instead. "Co" means "with," dependency means "I'm reliant on them."

In a codependent relationship, there is often more of a focus on the unhealthy person (who, in this scenario, we'll call "the addict") than on oneself (who we will call "the codependent"). Enormous amounts of time are spent trying to please or manage the addict and make sure they're okay. Most people who are in a relationship with an addict have low to no boundaries—all their energy goes to the addict and what they want. The addict will imply things like "I want you to let me do whatever I want. Don't require anything of me, no boundaries." Loyalty to the addict supersedes the codependent's health.

The underpinning of this dysfunction is not just unresolved or unhealed trauma but pain that is currently happening in the relationship. The addict is causing trauma to the codependent by requiring them to go along with, cover up, buy into lies, and make excuses for their toxic patterns, behaviors, addictions, and wrongdoings, causing damage to both parties.

Eventually this becomes a vicious cycle where both parties become unhealthy for many reasons but mostly because neither is committed to reality. Mental health is being committed to reality at all costs.

To check if you have codependent tendencies ask, "Is there a relationship in my life where I feel I can't be okay if I don't first work to make sure someone else is okay?"

Now, Let's Live This . . .

REMEMBER:

- Memories are both our greatest treasures and our greatest sorrows.
- Maybe the way we say goodbye can help us survive the memories.
- Even when people turned on Jesus, He didn't let a goodbye turn Him into someone He was never meant to be.
- Might it be possible to acknowledge hurt without unleashing hurt? Might it be possible to admit a necessary ending without unnecessary slander?
- I'd like a little more "God be with you" in my goodbyes.

RECEIVE:

The Lord says:

"These people come near to me with their mouth
    and honor me with their lips,
      but their hearts are far from me.
Their worship of me
    is based on merely human rules
they have been taught." (Isaiah 29:13)

The Spirit of the Sovereign Lord is on me,
    because the Lord has anointed me
    to proclaim good news to the poor.
He has sent me to bind up the brokenhearted,
    to proclaim freedom for the captives
    and release from darkness for the prisoners. (Isaiah 61:1)

REFLECT:

- What has your experience been like with necessary goodbyes? What was good and what was difficult about these experiences?
- How does it help you to know that saying goodbye can be biblical?
- Try the exercise I mentioned at the end of the chapter: In your mind start placing all the difficult or painful memories one by one into Jesus' strong, carpentry-calloused, nail-pierced, grace-gripped hands. Ask the Lord to help you whisper "God be with you" over each one. What memories do you need to release? What memories do you need to hold onto?

PRAYER:

God, You understand so very personally and deeply the heartache of watching someone you love walk away. As I look back at what was and look ahead at what will be, I know You are a refuge and safe place to process my feelings. Thank You for being so close to me during this time. I am looking to You and believing that today I can take some steps forward and whisper, "God be with you" to those who have left wounds in my heart. This isn't me saying I'm okay with what they did—I know You will eventually hold them accountable for their sin. But it is me saying I want to be okay again . . . better than okay. I want to fully live again. You can bring eventual good in all things, and today I trust that You absolutely will. In Jesus' name, amen.

CHAPTER 11

I'm Not Walking Away, I'm Accepting Reality

I've lived at the same address for thirty years. I've crossed the same threshold countless times with the comings and goings of all the major and minor happenings of my entire adult life. That one small line between the outside world and my family's safe place designated with some wood, bricks, and our very own front door. This one spot in this world has been witness to me carrying wedding gifts wrapped in paper, newborns wrapped in blankets, countless bags of groceries, balloons for parties, Band-Aids for boo boos, Easter dresses, prom dresses, and wedding gowns. I've also carried heartbreak, countless tissues full of tears, and whispered prayers of desperation in and out of that doorway.

I've rushed into that house with sheer excitement over finally being able to adopt our sons, getting my first real book deal, and seeing my kids come home safely after their first solo drive with a new license. I've also rushed out in sheer panic, taking kids to get stitches, trying to find one of our dogs that ran away, and finding evidence forcing me to face my greatest fears with someone I thought I could trust forever.

I've sat on those front steps and laughed, dreamed, wept, prayed, talked, screamed, processed, and taken thousands of deep breaths before walking back inside to my people.

So much life.

So many moments.

If I'm doing my math correctly, it's 60 seconds times 60 minutes times 24 hours times 365 days times 30 years, which totals 946,080,000 moments, give or take a few leap year days.

I've lived out my entire adult life returning to the same home base that saw me turn twenty-four, thirty-two, forty-five, and fifty-three years old.

Have you ever heard the expression that a house has "good bones"? Well, the bones are good in this place of mine in more than just a structural sense. It's been the sacred container of first words, first steps, and the raising up of my kids who I love most in this world. This home has taken me in. It's been the space that has dared to bear witness to the making and breaking of me. And when its walls and colors and some rooms full of tainted memories proved too triggering to leave in their original form, it survived being torn down to the original studs and proved that even the most bare-bones of the structure were still standing strong. The demolition and rebuilding of this house helped me see on the outside what was happening to me on the inside. So even in that process this house has been so good to me.

The house has had its issues at times, but I've held onto this safe haven that's held me all these years. I've stayed put.

I've been thinking about this a lot lately as I'm walking through the hardest goodbye I'll ever say. When the lump in my throat that has been there through years of unexpected heartbreak turned into an overwhelming heaviness in my chest, I could no longer deny the shift. I wasn't just in a difficult relationship. I was in an emotionally destructive relationship. I was told by three different counselors that if I didn't accept the ending before me, it would most likely mean the death of me.

I thought that to be a bit dramatic.

I shook my head in disbelief.

Not true, I thought. *Not true at all. I'm strong, I'm long-suffering. I'm loyal to a fault. My love is strong enough to withstand it all. I don't give up. I don't walk away. I won't walk away.*

So, I stayed. It seemed so right for a period of time. But then his old destructive habits returned, deceit infected conversations, and the biggest telltale sign of toxicity was I started feeling crazy again. When nothing makes sense, it is easy to lose all sense of reality. I didn't want the ending that all these choices seemed to be pointing to, so I did everything I could to stop it from happening. But that's like standing in front of a tornado with your hands out and believing you'll be able to redirect its vicious spin away from you. In the end, the tornado will suck you in, spit you out, and give no regard to how badly you are traumatized in the process.

What I didn't realize is that trauma isn't just something that happens to you. It happens in you. And the mistake I made is believing that I just needed to heal, forgive, and somehow move on from the facts of what happened. But emotional devastation isn't just a set of facts. The greater blow to your well-being is the *impact* all this has on you—how you feel, how you function, and how you think.

When thinking through a relationship that's shifted from difficult to destructive, we can't just consider the facts, we must consider the impact as well.

Like I taught in my book *Forgiving What You Can't Forget*, we

Trauma isn't just
something that
happens to you. It
happens in you.

— ugo

can make the choice to forgive the one who hurt us for the facts of what happened. But then we also must walk through the much longer process of forgiving and healing from the impact another person's actions have had on us. Forgiveness is a command by God, but reconciliation should be very conditional on many factors— most of all whether all parties involved can stay safe and healthy if they stay together.[1]

When healing from past emotional devastation, it's normal for the impact of what happened to present itself in the form of triggers. But what seriously tripped me up was thinking the alarm bells going off in my heart and mind were triggers from the past when in reality they were an indication of fresh trauma happening. New lies. New pain. New trauma. New denials. New confusion. New destruction.

Even so, I didn't want to walk away.

But then one day, as I was sitting in my house torn down to the studs with dust, debris, and chaos all around me, it suddenly occurred to me that I don't mind living through hard renovations because I always have a vision for something better that will surely come from all the hardship. Just like I could withstand the chaos of a renovation and still love this old house through it all, I can do that with people too. A renovation is a temporary setback that is actually a setup for something even more beautiful. There's a plan and when you stay true to the plan, you know what's being torn apart is for the purpose of being put back together better and stronger than before.

That was not the case in my marriage. There was a plan, but only I was staying true to the plan. Only I was staying put. We had mutually agreed to certain necessary boundaries, but he was no longer respecting them. All that we'd worked so hard to rebuild was now being torn apart. There's a big difference between a heart set on construction and one seemingly hell-bent on destruction.

I wasn't the one breaking away from relational health.

I wasn't the one breaking promises and breaking hearts.

I wasn't the one leaving the place we'd worked so hard to get to. And that's when I could finally say, "I'm not giving up. I'm not walking away. I'm choosing to finally accept reality."

ACCEPTING REALITY

Jim has probably reminded me more than a hundred times: "Mental health is a commitment to reality at all costs." I don't know what reality you need to accept right now. Maybe you have an easier time with that than I do. Or maybe, your reality isn't as heavy and hard as the one I just described. A big part of setting boundaries in even the best of circumstances is accepting the reality that when you know a change needs to happen, you need to move toward making it happen. You don't have to make all the changes at once. And you don't have to start with the biggest change.

But whatever reality is telling you, and however the Lord is leading you, move toward that. And that's exactly what we've been doing throughout this whole book.

And if reality is telling you that you've done all you can do, what comes next? You've made the big changes, you've prayed, you've sought wise counsel, you've had the conversations, you've set the boundaries, you've implemented the consequences, you've set even more clearly defined boundaries and yet, it's not working.

The neighbor is still showing up at your house "borrowing" things out of your garage without asking.
The family member is still coming to gatherings drunk.
The friend is still making unrealistic demands and berating you for not doing what they want.
The coworker is still stealing from the cash drawer and expecting you to cover for them.

The guy you are dating who says he's a committed believer is
   still making inappropriate comments and trying to make
   you feel guilty for not sleeping with him.
The spouse is still lying, hiding their secret devices, and
   refusing to give an account for the mysterious charges on
   the credit card.
The friend who helps organize the neighborhood playgroup
   is still allowing her kids to bully and belittle your child
   with no consequences and acts like it's no big deal.

Remember all the work you've done to draw boundaries was
not about controlling someone else's behavior. It's about paying
attention and being honest about how someone's poor behavior and
lack of responsibility is possibly controlling you. And when people
close to us are acting out of control, that's when we run the greatest
risk of lacking self-control.

When a relationship shifts from being difficult to being
destructive, it's the right time to consider a goodbye. Here's how
Christian counselor Leslie Vernick defines the difference between
difficult and destructive relationships:

My definition of an emotionally destructive relationship is this:
Pervasive and repetitive patterns of actions and attitudes that
result in tearing someone down or inhibiting a person's growth,
often accompanied by a lack of awareness, lack of remorse and
lack of change.[2]

In another article specifically about marriage, Leslie states:

God tells us that bullies, abusers, and oppressors do exist in
this world. But he also clearly tells us that they are never to be
protected, sanctioned, or supported by God's people, especially

within an intimate relationship (Ephesians 5:25 AMP; Colossians 3:19 AMP) . . . The marital relationship is the most intimate relationship God has ordained. In God's design for marriage, being married should never lead to less safety, less sanity, or less strengthening for the individuals in that relationship but rather continue to nurture and nourish those qualities. Safety and trust are the most important foundation to maintain a healthy marriage.[3]

Though Leslie was specifically talking about marriage here, I think her wisdom should be considered for all relationships. When we give people relational access to us, it should never lead to "less safety, less sanity, or less strengthening for the individuals in that relationship."

Remember boundaries don't work when we continue to give too much access to people who aren't being responsible with that access. And when their level of responsibility is a zero, their level of access to you should also be a zero.

When this is the case, God's not disappointed in you saying goodbye.

Actually, God modeled this. And we should follow His lead.

God actually established this from the beginning of time.

Remember, like we discussed in chapter 4, when God communicated the first boundary with Adam in the garden of Eden, He started the boundary conversation with "You are free . . ." They were free to eat from any of the fruit trees in the garden except the fruit of the tree of the knowledge of good and evil. God was clear: if you live in My holy garden, you have lots of freedom but you will not bring sin into this place. When Adam and Eve brought sin in, they demonstrated they didn't have enough responsibility to be allowed continued access to the garden of Eden, which is also where they had direct access to God.

God didn't just make them leave the garden, He made sure to put up guards so they couldn't ever return. This was in part because Adam and Eve had sinned. The garden was the equivalent to what would eventually become the holy of holies in the temple. God is holy. And wherever God resides is a holy place. Therefore, without the blood of Jesus to cover their sin, Adam and Eve were utterly exposed and the most vulnerable they'd ever been. Remember, generations later when the temple is established, if a high priest went into the holy of holies without being completely purified from their sin, they would drop dead. Adam and Eve were the high priests of the garden of Eden. Their eyes had been opened to evil. They had the taste of it on their tongue. And they had unleashed the consequences of that choice. Tragically, their sin separated them from God and ended the perfection with Him they once enjoyed. Not only were their bodies now aging toward death and physically decaying, but they had opened their souls up to corruption as well. The pull of the enemy would forever be to entice people's hearts toward sin and death. The pull of God would forever be toward inviting people into holiness and life. The darkness of sin could not then coexist with the pure light of God's holiness.

But there was another reason Adam and Eve had to leave the garden, as we discussed earlier in the book. If they had continued to have access to the garden, they may have then eaten from the tree of life. Eating the fruit of that tree of life gave the recipient eternal life (Genesis 3:22). Think about that. Adam and Eve would have forever been stuck in a state of their sin's depravity and separation from God Himself.

God wanted redemption for Adam and Eve. . . . therefore, He didn't enable them. He didn't excuse away the problem they created. He didn't make an exception and hope for the best. He didn't allow them to keep sinning in His sacred garden. No, He let them face the consequences of their own choices. He responded to the choice they made and put them out of the garden. It was necessary to end their access to the garden.

They demonstrated zero responsibility in the garden, therefore their access to the garden was taken away.

God didn't abandon Adam and Eve, but their relationship dramatically changed. God no longer provided a perfect environment where gardening was immediately fruitful. Now, Adam would have to work hard to get the ground to produce food and sometimes his gardening efforts would all be in vain. Adam and Eve no longer had the same kind of provision, power, and authority they once had in the garden. And they and their descendants would forever wrestle between giving in to the pull of the flesh or surrendering to better choices that lead to God's peace (1 Corinthians 10:13).

We are all still suffering the consequences of Adam and Eve. But the good news is, we have a choice to regain the peace once lost to Adam and Eve. Romans 8:5–6 says, "Those who live according to the flesh have their minds set on what the flesh desires; but those who live in accordance with the Spirit have their minds set on what the Spirit desires. The mind governed by the flesh is death, but the mind governed by the Spirit is life and peace."

We can also look at Colossians 3:1–5, which reminds us to set our hearts and minds on things above since we are in Christ, which requires us to "put to death, therefore, whatever belongs to your earthly nature: sexual immorality, impurity, lust, evil desires and greed, which is idolatry."

"Put to death" means we take daily action to continually rid ourselves of sinful attitudes, desires, choices, and habits. Boundaries are crucial in living out these verses. If we are working to keep our minds and hearts free from the entanglements of sin, then when people are participating in sinful activities around us, the sin should no longer be enabled by us.

Now, this doesn't mean we can't love someone who is in active sin. But it does mean we don't participate in what they choose to do. And we don't allow their choices to harm us and start drawing our heart into places of compromise, devastation, or deception.

Again, we all need grace when we mess up. But we also need the awareness that there is a difference between an occasional slip in behavior and an ongoing pattern of behavior. Let's be completely honest with ourselves and those who can help us discern what's the best way to respond and move toward healing. If healing is possible together, then take that path toward peace. But if healing isn't possible if you stay in relationship with this person, then take a separate path toward peace.

Please hear me—I know this is complicated and heartbreaking and should never be taken lightly. I'm not advocating we throw away friends and family members when things get tough. I have always felt passionate about leaving room for God to move in the other person's heart and in mine. We don't want to live in the extremes of rushing what shouldn't be rushed. And I'm certainly not advocating a quick and easy pathway to ghosting friends, no longer seeing your parents, or quickly divorcing your spouse. Processing a possible goodbye isn't permission to peace out or tap out. It's a pathway toward grieving and accepting one of the toughest realities we will ever face—an unsustainable relationship.

Those words *unsustainable relationship* feel like a stab to my heart. I want relationships to be good and last for good. The grief over relationships ending is some of the deepest I've ever known. At times, this kind of loss can seem worse than death. Other times an ending has brought relief from the turmoil and toxicity of that relationship, so it's no longer a daily battle. But even then, my heart breaks over the reconciliation and redemption story I had hoped would be possible.

There is a verse that's tripped me up at times because my heart is so very hopeful that it is possible to reach a place of peace with

Processing a possible goodbye isn't permission to peace out or tap out. It's a pathway toward grieving and accepting one of the toughest realities we will ever face—an unsustainable relationship.

everyone. Romans 12:18: "If possible, so far as it depends on you, live peaceably with all" (ESV). In my marriage, I wrongly thought that eventually I could do enough, pray enough, give in enough, rescue enough, or make myself change for him enough, and finally an equilibrium of peace could be reached. But that's not what this verse means. I guess I missed those first couple of words Paul intentionally used with this verse, "if possible," which imply sometimes it is *not* possible. Charles Spurgeon, one of the most famous preachers in the 1800s, once taught on this verse in a way that now helps me have better sense with insensible people:

> In the Jardin des Plantes we saw a hooded snake in a most unamiable condition of temper. There was a thick glass and a stout wire between us, and we did nothing but look at him, yet he persisted in darting at us with the utmost vehemence of malice, until the keeper requested us to move away, with the advice that it was not well to irritate such creatures. When one meets with an irascible person, on the look out to pick a quarrel, ill-conditioned, and out of elbows with the whole world, it is best to move on, and let him alone. Even if he can do you no harm, and if his irritation be utterly unreasonable, it is best to remove all exciting causes of provocation, for it is never wise to irritate vipers. You do not on purpose walk heavily across the floor to

teach a gouty man that you have no respect for his tender feelings since he ought not to be so susceptible; neither should you vex those afflicted with a bad temper, and then plead that they have no right to be so excitable. If our neighbours' tempers are gunpowder, let us not play with fire.[4]

Notice that the viper in Spurgeon's story was behind glass. There was a boundary. And notice that they weren't provoking the viper, they were just looking at him. That means the irritation and desire to strike was inside of the snake. The snake's lack of peace on the outside was because of his own lack of peace on the inside. If there was something that the people were doing to disrupt the snake's peace, then it would have been possible to stop their actions and peace would return. But the keeper of the snake knew that there would be no peace for the onlookers until they moved away from the snake. Their presence, not their problems, was causing the snake to be so irritated that he was striking at the people. And without that glass boundary between them, whether the snake intended to harm the people or not, the impact of a viper's bite is still poisonous.

Spurgeon goes on to equate this viper to people whose irritation is utterly unreasonable. They don't have peace on the inside, therefore it probably won't be possible for them to live with a consistency of peace on the outside. People who cause harm emotionally, physically, socially, sexually, financially, spiritually, intellectually, or relationally, whether they intend to or not, have a toxic impact on those who do life with them. Notice, I didn't say those who make mistakes and then repent and get help to not make those mistakes again. But when those who inflict harm aren't horrified by it enough to get help so they don't do it again, they most likely will do it again. And remember, the greater access we give them, the greater we will feel the impact of their harmful actions and the longer it will take us to recover from it all.

If we want recovery and healing, we would be wise to take a break or possibly make a clean break from the one wounding us. When saying goodbye . . .

We can do it without hatred (anger) like God instructs.

> Be angry and do not sin; do not let the sun go down on your anger. (Ephesians 4:26 ESV)

We can do it for a season or do it for a lifetime like God instructs.

> A time to search and a time to give up,
> a time to keep and a time to throw away. (Ecclesiastes 3:6)

We can have compassion on their pain like God instructs.

> Even in darkness light dawns for the upright,
> for those who are gracious and compassionate and
> righteous. (Psalm 112:4)

We can and should work to forgive them like God instructs.

> Be kind to one another, tenderhearted, forgiving one another, as God in Christ forgave you. (Ephesians 4:32 ESV)

We can get rid of bitterness toward them like God instructs.

> See to it that no one fails to obtain the grace of God; that no "root of bitterness" springs up and causes trouble, and by it many become defiled. (Hebrews 12:15 ESV)

If we want recovery and

healing, we would be wise

to take a break or possibly

make a clean break from

the one wounding us.

— Lyss

Get rid of all bitterness, rage and anger, brawling and slander, along with every form of malice. (Ephesians 4:31)

We can keep praying for them like God instructs.

"But I tell you, love your enemies and pray for those who persecute you." (Matthew 5:44)

. . . And we can move on from them like God instructs.

People will be lovers of themselves, lovers of money, boastful, proud, abusive, disobedient to their parents, ungrateful, unholy, without love, unforgiving, slanderous, without self-control, brutal, not lovers of the good, treacherous, rash, conceited, lovers of pleasure rather than lovers of God—having a form of godliness but denying its power. Have nothing to do with such people. (2 Timothy 3:2–5)

None of this is easy to process. And a decision to say goodbye should not be made in a rush without wise counsel and much prayer. But remember, although God loved people so much that He gave His only Son's life to try and save us, He's also willing to accept our refusal to be saved. God has a line that He will not allow to be crossed. If someone refuses salvation, they will not be rewarded with eternal access to Him.

Let's take another look at Hebrews 12:14–15: "Strive for peace with everyone, and for the holiness without which no one will see the Lord. See to it that no one fails to obtain the grace of God; that no 'root of bitterness' springs up and causes trouble, and by it many become defiled" (ESV).

If peace isn't possible in the current circumstances in a relationship, then we must strive to find peace with that person by changing the circumstances or changing the relationship. We must remember that the longer a destructive relationship stays in turmoil and unhealth, the greater the risk will be for bitterness to creep in. And bitterness doesn't just cause trouble for the person feeling it, it has a negative impact on and defiles all those around it.

Here are more Bible verses containing God's wisdom that we should factor into our thoughts and prayers when considering a goodbye.

> The perverse of heart shall be far from me;
>   I will have nothing to do with what is evil.
> Whoever slanders their neighbor in secret,
>   I will put to silence;
> whoever has haughty eyes and a proud heart,
>   I will not tolerate. (Psalm 101:4–5)

> No one who practices deceit
>   will dwell in my house;
> no one who speaks falsely
>   will stand in my presence. (Psalm 101:7)

Warn a divisive person once, and then warn them a second time. After that, have nothing to do with them. You may be sure that such people are warped and sinful; they are self-condemned. (Titus 3:10–11)

> Acquitting the guilty and condemning the innocent—
>   the LORD detests them both. (Proverbs 17:15)

But if the unbeliever leaves, let it be so. The brother or the sister is not bound in such circumstances; God has called us to live in peace. (1 Corinthians 7:15)

I urge you, brothers and sisters, to watch out for those who cause divisions and put obstacles in your way that are contrary to the teaching you have learned. Keep away from them. (Romans 16:17)

So, what do we do about the grief all of this causes us? We will talk about that in the next chapter. And is there a way to say goodbye without completely cutting someone out of our lives? In some cases yes, and we will talk about that as well.

But for now, let's park on why we must do what we've probably been avoiding doing for a very long time. Is it just to have more peace? Is it just so we don't get bitter? Is it so we don't get pulled into endorsing activities and behaviors we don't agree with? Is it just a way to stop the harm and start the healing? All of those things are part of it.

However, there's one more really important factor. Remember my house and how I had it torn down to the studs to fix it so it could function better and be built back stronger and more beautiful? It's done now. The debris is gone. The brokenness is gone. The chaos is gone.

When I walk into my space now, it feels fully alive.

And that's what I want to be too.

As the second-century church father Irenaeus said, "The glory of God is a human fully alive."[5] True, Jesus did say, "Whoever wants to be my disciple must deny themselves and take up their cross daily and follow me" (Luke 9:23). But when we apply this verse rigidly, without qualification from the rest of Scripture, it leads to the very opposite of what God intends. We are to die to the sinful parts of who we are. "We are not called by God to die to the 'good' parts of who we are. God never asked us to die to the healthy desires and pleasures of life—to friendships, joy, art, music, beauty, recreation, laughter, and nature."[6]

So, with that I exhale my sorrow. And for the first time in a long while I dare to inhale the courage I know God will surely give me. I open my front door and cross my old threshold with new possibilities to be me—healthy, whole, and fully alive.

A note from Jim on goodbyes

There's a big difference between waiting for a breaking point and establishing a breaking point. A goodbye shouldn't sneak up on us because if we set boundaries with consequences, breaking points are established ahead of time. As boundary violations occur, there will be changes in the relationship so that you can protect yourself from hurtful patterns and behaviors that you are no longer willing to tolerate.

Establishing a breaking point can sometimes be a boundary that helps the relationship stay healthy. It clears up the nebulous questions around what is and is not permitted between you and the other person. That clarity will make the need for a goodbye much more obvious to both parties.

It is helpful to think through boundary limits and breaking points when you are in a nonemotional, nonconfrontational mental space. Remember, like we talked about before, it's important to prepare in times of security for times of insecurity. It's important to prepare in times of health for times of dysfunction. So, here are a few questions to help you identify what a breaking point is for you:

- What am I willing to live with?
- What is and is not acceptable behavior?
- What are my deal breakers that would pull me from a place of health into unhealth?

Now, Let's Live This . . .

REMEMBER:

- Trauma isn't just something that happens to you. It happens in you.
- When thinking through a relationship that's shifted from difficult to destructive, we can't just consider the facts, we must consider the impact as well.
- When people close to us are acting out of control, that's when we run the greatest risk of lacking self-control.
- Processing a possible goodbye isn't permission to peace out or tap out. It's a pathway toward grieving and accepting one of the toughest realities we will ever face—an unsustainable relationship.
- If we want recovery and healing, we would be wise to take a break or possibly make a clean break from the one wounding us.
- We don't want to violate God's Word in our efforts to keep God's Word.

RECEIVE:

Those who live according to the flesh have their minds set on what the flesh desires; but those who live in accordance with the Spirit have their minds set on what the Spirit desires. The mind governed by the flesh is death, but the mind governed by the Spirit is life and peace. (Romans 8:5–6)

If possible, so far as it depends on you, live peaceably with all. (Romans 12:18 ESV)

But mark this: There will be terrible times in the last days. People will be lovers of themselves, lovers of money, boastful, proud, abusive, disobedient to their parents, ungrateful, unholy, without love, unforgiving, slanderous, without self-control, brutal, not lovers of the good, treacherous, rash, conceited, lovers of pleasure rather than lovers of God—having a form of godliness but denying its power. Have nothing to do with such people. (2 Timothy 3:1–5)

I urge you, brothers and sisters, to watch out for those who cause divisions and put obstacles in your way that are contrary to the teaching you have learned. Keep away from them. (Romans 16:17)

REFLECT:

- Is there a certain relationship in your life that would benefit from you accepting reality? What might this change for you?
- How does the following sentence apply to your life right now? "If peace isn't possible in the current circumstances in a relationship, then we must strive to find peace with that person by changing the circumstances or changing the relationship."
- How have you misunderstood what it means to deny yourself, take up your cross daily, and follow Jesus (Luke 9:23)?

PRAYER:

God, sometimes it's really hard to accept things in front of me that I cannot change. But I am so confident in Your perfect ability to be God. You are the only One who can bring real change in my life. As I pray through some relationship adjustments I may have to make, including goodbyes, I pray You would give me holy discernment and wisdom as I make any decisions. Show me who I can trust to process some of these things with. Thank You for Your never-ending love and faithfulness toward me. I know You will never leave me. In Jesus' name, amen.

CHAPTER 12

A Million Little Funerals

Is it possible to say goodbye without cutting this person out of my life completely? Is it possible for me to just take a break for a season of healing but not break ties with them completely? Is there a way to regain peace with this person even if I still don't agree with them, approve of their choices, or understand how they are choosing to live their lives? What if this is a difficult relationship but not a destructive one? What if I'm just not ready to say goodbye but I do want to reduce the emotional access they have to me? What if they still aren't sensitive to my feelings, constantly disappoint me, or don't live up to the dreams I always had for us but they aren't causing me harm, what possibilities for change are there?

These are the questions you might have with some of your relationships. Especially if it really isn't possible to reduce someone's physical access to you.

Let's think about it like this. Have you ever been on the phone around dinnertime with someone who is on the west coast while you are on the east coast? You are talking in real time on the very same day. But your day now looks vastly different from their day. You've already gotten home from work, watched the sunset, eaten dinner, and started winding down for the evening. Meanwhile, the person on the west coast is just gearing up for another meeting at work, the sun is as bright as ever, and they are still full from lunch.

What a difference it is for someone whose watch reads 7:30 p.m. EST and another whose watch says 4:30 p.m. PST.

You are both living in the same day but are in two totally different places. And even if you wanted to be on the phone together watching the sunset, that wouldn't be possible unless they travel toward you a great distance or you travel toward them a great distance. If neither of you can do that, then you may have to let go of watching the sunset at the same time. It doesn't make either of you bad people, it just means you aren't in the same place.

This applies to where we live. But it also applies to relational differences in how we live.

As we talked about before, sometimes there's a gap that exposes those relational differences and makes them so much more obvious. As you move through life, if you are committed to developing humility, growing in spiritual maturity, staying emotionally and physically healthy, and managing your relationships more wisely, you're going to find those gaps ever-widening between where you are and where some of those around you are. If others have refused to go to counseling, as you learn healthier ways to process what you face, it's only natural that unhealthy conversations will start to feel odd and uncomfortable. When you are looking into God's Word for guidance, those who look elsewhere won't feel as grounded. And as you've done the good work of forgiveness, those still holding onto grudges will frustrate you.

It's so hard to recognize what *is* when you've been persistently trying to get someone to step into what *could be*. You can see it so clearly. It's 7:30 EST to you. But it's still just 4:30 PST to them. And unless you can alter the universe and wrangle the sun, you just aren't going to be able to get your vision and their vision to align.

And chances are it will make you cry. Not because they are missing the sunset, but because you're both going to miss out on what could have been. It will all seem so senseless.

It will seem so senseless when your biological dad doesn't treasure you or have the desire to protect you as you see your friends' dads doing for them. You've dreamed of having conversations with him where you know he'd do anything for you. Instead, he acts rushed like you might be a bit of an inconvenience to him.

It will seem so heartbreaking when you get to the place with your mom, grandmother, or even a close friend that you fear her verbal attacks if you think or do something differently than she would. You want her to be a source of wisdom for you. But instead, you now have to avoid sharing vulnerable thoughts with her or run the risk of her crushing you with her opinions and unrealistic expectations.

I get it. When I so very much keep wanting and hoping for someone to say something they've never said or do something they've never done, I've now decided to accept that maybe they never will.

And I've survived. I've more than survived.

I let grief into that raw space. And the very grief I've spent years avoiding actually helped me move forward. I thought that only a particular person could fill my empty place of unmet longing. But when I let grief in, what had felt numb for so long came alive in waves of honesty:

He hadn't ever truly protected me.

She hadn't ever really listened to me.

Grief made me face my disappointment. Grief made me realize that my sadness wasn't because I was wanting dead things to come back to life. I kept crying because my basic desires had never been given life in the first place.

I didn't have epic expectations. They were normal things that healthy relationships need in order to survive. I wanted to feel safe. I wanted to feel heard. I wanted to feel I could believe what the person was saying was actually true. And I wanted to know they had my best interest in mind just like I had their best interest in mind.

I had to own the fact that I loved these people for who I thought they would be as a spouse, a family member, a friend, or a coworker, instead of who they actually were. I loved the idea of them loving me well but not how they actually treated me. I had hopes for these people and these relationships that they didn't have at all. I think we can all form pictures in our minds of the roles other people fulfill in our lives. But it's utterly unhelpful for us to point fingers at them and try to make them change. And the longer we do this, the more we will miss getting to know and acknowledge who they really are.

I would never be able to draw appropriate boundaries with this person while holding onto my made-up version of them. The problem wasn't that they didn't see my vision for them. The real problem was I had refused to see them as they really are.

Grief helped me understand the death before me. I had to let go of that picture in my mind I've clung to and cried over, stared at and sulked over. I had to stop inviting them to dinner expecting them to show up and be like my desired version of them only to be crushed once again by their uncaring words and actions. They never had that eye-opening breakthrough while passing the gravy past the wildflower centerpiece. Never ever.

Washing the dishes later by myself, there was nothing but coldness and emptiness and frustration that as I set the table that night, I'd once again set myself up for sadness. Grief kept knocking. And when I finally let it in everything got a little clearer and I finally knew what I had to do. I had to put the unrealistic picture of this person and this relationship into the flame of grief. And plan a funeral.

Sometimes these funerals will lead to a renewed relationship.

When previous expectations fade away we can finally see who the other person really is. Maybe it's not everything we hoped for but there is something we can like. A new start.

Sometimes these funerals will lead to a temporary pause when you don't communicate or see each other for a while but eventually come back together. A chance to slowly rebuild after a safe season of separation.

Other times, they will lead to a final, forever goodbye to the relationship you once had. An ending.

I wish I could give you a formula so you could calculate whether it will ever be healthy or wise to reconnect with this person. I may or may not have googled to see if such a formula exists. I couldn't find one.

Instead, I've tried to approach each situation with its own unique dynamics and make a healthy determination of what to do using the wisdom I've learned from God's Word, trusted counsel, and the discernment of the Holy Spirit. It can feel messy. We might not always get it right. And for a 2 + 2 = 4, rule-follower girl like me that's a hard reality to accept long term. I just want to know the right thing to do and I want doing the right thing to lead to predictable happiness.

So, I'm having to make peace with the fact there isn't a formula to calculate where the relationship will go next. There will be some renewed relationships. There will be some temporary pauses. And there will be some forever goodbyes. But what is consistent with every one of these scenarios? Grief.

You will probably cry to varying degrees with each direction a strained relationship may go in.

I love deeply. So, I tend to hurt just as deeply. And the only way I know to mark where the hurting ends and the healing begins is with a funeral.

I'm not sure how many funerals like this I've planned. But just to keep willing myself to do them, I say to myself there's going to be a million little funerals in my life that no one else attends. And it will probably be that way in your life too. And no one is going to bring you flowers and a casserole. There are Tuesday morning funerals and Friday night funerals and 7:30 p.m. sunset-after-work funerals. There are funerals that happen when you're brushing your teeth or pouring a cup of coffee or making that drive you could do in your sleep. It's not complicated or long or encapsulated within a perfectly crafted speech.

It's incredibly basic. And, for me, it's incredibly helpful.

So, here's how one of these funerals goes for me:

1. I acknowledge what isn't.
2. I state out loud what makes me so disappointed and how unfair the whole situation feels. I see it as a good thing to cry out to God. I will get it all out because He can handle my honesty, fear, anger, and utter devastation expressed in its most raw form.
3. I give myself permission to cry as many tears as I need to.
4. I then uninvite the image of the person I've held onto. That picture of who I wanted them to be isn't reality. That picture isn't reality. That picture isn't reality.
5. I acknowledge the person is unwilling or incapable of what I so very much desire for them and our relationship. But my desire doesn't line up with their desire. So, it's not realistic at this time.
6. I release the person to be responsible for her life, just as I'm responsible for my life.
7. I allow myself some time to feel sad and experience the emotions of grief.
8. I say out loud what I'm releasing. "I am choosing to let go of _____" (for example, resentment, anger, bitterness).

The only way I know to

mark where the hurting

ends and the healing

begins is with a funeral.

— *Ugo*

9. I say out loud what this will now allow me space to receive. "I am choosing to receive _____" (for example, joy, hope, a better future).
10. I commit to setting and maintaining good boundaries for myself.
11. And I will have another funeral about this tomorrow if need be.

We are powerless to stop grief from happening. It will visit us all in various forms and for many different reasons. But the absolute commonality for all grief is the disappointment and pain that accompanies it. We mourn what will not be. But even more so we mourn what imperfection and sin has done to all of us. We all contribute to the reasons there is so much pain in this world. We all hurt others. We all fall short in the roles and responsibilities we carry. We all cause grief. We all carry grief.

But the good news is, we don't have to be consumed by our grief.

Isaiah 53:2–6 is very comforting to me when I remember that I don't carry all this grief alone. Jesus bore our grief—both the grief we cause and the grief we endure. And He provides healing and hope for us all. I love how Eugene Peterson personalizes what Jesus did in this paraphrase of that passage:

> The servant grew up before God—a scrawny seedling,
>   a scrubby plant in a parched field.
> There was nothing attractive about him,
>   nothing to cause us to take a second look.
> He was looked down on and passed over,
>   a man who suffered, who knew pain firsthand.
> One look at him and people turned away.
>   We looked down on him, thought he was scum.
> But the fact is, it was our pains he carried—

our disfigurements, all the things wrong with us.
We thought he brought it on himself,
    that God was punishing him for his own failures.
But it was our sins that did that to him,
    that ripped and tore and crushed him—*our sins*!
He took the punishment, and that made us whole.
    Through his bruises we get healed.
We're all like sheep who've wandered off and gotten lost.
    We've all done our own thing, gone our own way.
And God has piled all our sins,
everything we've done wrong,
    on him, on him. (THE MESSAGE)

So, the last part of my funeral is bringing it all to Jesus. The grief. The pain. The longings unfulfilled. My sin against them. Their sin against me. My need for forgiveness. And the forgiveness I need to offer. I ask Him to stand in the gap between where I am and where I long to be. I give to Him what I now know won't be and ask Him to bring His fullness into my emptiness.

And I just let it be.

If I need to cry, I cry.

If I need to journal, I journal.

If I need to write it all out on paper and tear it up into hundreds of pieces, I do.

If I need to then talk it all out with my counselor or a friend, I pick up the phone.

But the one thing I don't do is go back to pretending and living in denial. I've accepted this grief. I've had the marked moment of accepting what is and what is not. And it's from this place of acceptance that I will move forward into healing.

I was processing this with my friend Madi, who is learning to have her own million little funerals that are all pointing to different outcomes. One night we were sitting on the front stoop drinking apple cider. This was one of the items on her fall bucket list. Note to self, I need some seasonal bucket lists in my life. Madi said, "What's ahead has to be better than what's behind. God isn't going to take me somewhere worse than where I've already been." Then she questioned herself, "Is that really true though?"

I took another sip and kept thinking about that question. The next morning, I replied, "I think the answer to your question is yes and no. No, because God may allow and probably will allow more hardships ahead. Yes, because all that you've already faced in your life has strengthened you to face what's ahead with more resiliency and assurance that God will take everything and work good from it (2 Corinthians 4:17–18). You aren't that same unsure and vulnerable girl today that you were ten years ago. You've allowed what you've faced to strengthen you instead of weakening you. You are wiser. You are more discerning. You are more assured of how to stay close to God. So, you'll go with God more readily and see His goodness ahead more quickly. Start having your funerals, marked moments of closure, and you'll see. This one will better prepare you for the next one. And that one for the one after that."

This is true for Madi. It's true for me. And it's true for you, too, my friend. As we better grieve the sorrows, we will soon receive our tomorrows with a little more healing and a lot more life.

> "Forget the former things;
>> do not dwell on the past.
> See, I am doing a new thing!
>> Now it springs up; do you not perceive it?
> I am making a way in the wilderness
>> and streams in the wasteland." (Isaiah 43:18–19)

As we better grieve the sorrows, we will soon receive our tomorrows with a little more healing and a lot more life.

A note from Jim on the grieving process

Going through the grieving process and having funerals for relationships is hard, but it's healthy and beneficial for many reasons, including the following:

1. Helps you get closure. Grieving a relationship is a personal experience and not dependent on the other person.
2. Allows you to release what was real, what wasn't real, and what will never be the same again.
3. Creates a space to feel the loss of investing many years of your life in a relationship that didn't unfold the way you wanted, nor did it last a lifetime as you'd hoped.
4. Allows you to finally let go of the person you thought they were, but also to consider who you were with that person. This creates an opportunity to ask some internal questions, such as, "What did I miss early on that should have been a red flag?" "What did I tolerate for too long?" "What parts of myself did I lose that I want to get back?"

5. Helps you get to a better place before new layers and waves of grief come. For example, facing the reality that the spouse you divorced or the friend you let go of may be validated and even celebrated by others as a great person when that wasn't your experience at all.

6. Helps ensure you begin to heal, because what you don't work out, you'll act out. Unhealed grief will spill, or sometimes even spew, onto other people— our kids, family members, friends—and can even contribute to long-term mental health issues.

Now, Let's Live This . . .

REMEMBER:

- When we love deeply, we tend to hurt just as deeply.
- The only way I know to mark where the hurting ends and the healing begins is with a funeral.
- We are powerless to stop grief from happening. It will visit us all in various forms and for many different reasons.
- As we better grieve the sorrows, we will soon receive our tomorrows with a little more healing and a lot more life.

RECEIVE:

For our light and momentary troubles are achieving
for us an eternal glory that far outweighs them
all. So we fix our eyes not on what is seen, but on
what is unseen, since what is seen is temporary,
but what is unseen is eternal. (2 Corinthians
4:17–18)

He took the punishment, and that made us whole.
Through his bruises we get healed. (Isaiah 53:5 THE
MESSAGE)

REFLECT:

- Is there a specific person who comes to mind as you think about letting go of your idea of them? What funeral or marked moment of closure do you need to help you grieve?
- In what ways can you see this process of learning to grieve helping you in your life circumstances and relationships?

PRAYER:

Heavenly Father, please comfort my heart through all the grief I'm feeling. Please help me through any "little funerals" I may need to process and pray through. On the other side of hurting and healing, I pray for supernatural joy. I know the story You're writing for my life is so much better than any story I could ever write for myself. I know You still have good things in store for my life and my relationships. When my circumstances are uncertain and unpredictable, I will declare my absolute trust in You above it all. In Jesus' name, amen.

Conclusion

A Bible, a Ring, and a God
Who Never Leaves Us

I can't believe we are turning some of the final pages of this book. I'm glad we've walked through this message together. I think we've both discovered that boundaries aren't the quick fix that maybe we hoped they would be for some of our most challenging relationships. People are complicated. We are complicated. So, of course, relationships are going to be complicated. But the communication and consistency that good boundaries provide bring such clarity around what to do when damaging dysfunctions are present.

Are boundaries still going to be challenging? Yes. But at least we know what to do even if it's still sometimes hard. The worst part of dysfunction in relationships is the feeling of hopelessness and powerlessness that too many of us have been swirling in for years.

Knowing what to do with challenging relationships is the greatest gift we've discovered in this book. I'm more convinced than ever that good boundaries work. When set appropriately and kept consistently, boundaries really do serve to help keep us safe and our relationships healthy.

During the writing of this book, I've established some healthy

boundaries and, as a result, had some really important relationships transform and become healthier and lifegiving to both me
and those I love. I'm amazed and thankful. There's a freedom to
enjoy these relationships now without the hesitations and pitfalls
that used to create so much chaos and pain.

One of those relationships that comes to mind is a close friend
who has a strong personality and can talk with great intensity.
Sometimes this helps me. Other times, it upsets me. And sometimes
my gentler and less direct approach frustrates her. But, as we have
walked through seasons of boundary failures with each other, we
have learned just how important it is to remember three things: to
communicate the boundaries we need, to remind each other of those
boundaries (especially when one of us gets too relaxed in respecting
them), and to not make everything a huge deal. Sometimes we need
to have a discussion. Other times, we just need a reminder of why
these parameters are important. And ultimately, we give each other
grace and keep on going. I think all of this has proven to take our
relationship the distance.

In years past, without boundaries, I probably would have
distanced myself from this person because I didn't know how to
handle the strength with which she says or does things. But now,
with boundaries, I have the tools necessary to protect my vulnera-
bilities without constantly criticizing her strengths. Our friendship
has become richer because of boundaries. And as we navigate our
differences in healthy ways, we are both becoming better because
of what we've worked through together.

But during the writing of this book, I also had to say a goodbye
I never wanted. A goodbye that still feels hard to believe some days.
A goodbye that was messy and maddening and so very confusing.
And yet, it was also so very necessary.

Maybe you've experienced both the beauty of good boundaries
and the heartbreaking realities of a goodbye in this season of your

> When set appropriately and kept consistently, boundaries really do serve to help keep us safe and our relationships healthy.

life as well. I hope you've felt less alone because you picked up this book. Sometimes what gets me through the hardest parts of my life is knowing I'm not the only one going through it.

You may feel lonely, but you aren't alone. And though I can't see your face right now, I've pictured you in the writing of every one of these words, which helped me not feel alone as well. I was so grateful and so comforted knowing you were out there and this book would bring our journeys together. So, as much as I hope you've been helped, I've been helped too.

By the time you read this, a year will have passed from what I'm about to share happened for me. But today, for me, it's the freshest heartbreak and breakthrough of this entire process.

This week, two emails arrived to my inbox within hours of each other. One was the "Word of the Day." Being a girl who works with words, processes life by writing words, and loves learning new words, I enjoy this daily email. Most of the time I've never heard of the word and I don't have a clue what it means. But on this day, the word was *poignant*—evoking a keen sense of sadness or regret. It comes from the Latin verb *pungere*, meaning "to prick or sting."[1]

I knew that word. I had been living with a keen sense of sadness for years over the unraveling of my marriage, my most important human relationship. The pain was deep. The shock of things I never thought would happen were unfolding in front of me and my children, and it was almost too much to bear. The hope of things getting better was almost too good to be true. And then the devastation of realizing that the relationship couldn't be reconciled left me with hundreds of unanswered questions and a pillow soaked with tears.

The next email was from my attorney. It was the divorce papers. It was absolutely a moment that pricked and stung. I guess it was poignant. Another stab in the deepest part of my heart.

I was facing the end of what I had promised would be forever. But I couldn't be the only one to keep those sacred vows and have a marriage that honored God. So many people asked me why I stayed and fought for my marriage. There were honorable reasons. But there were unhealthy reasons too. I've had to do the long therapeutic work of disentangling myself from unknowingly being a codepend-ent rescuer who in the end realized how futile my efforts were in the face of addictions and choices that were not mine to own.

But though I'd had good intentions with my grace and love, I finally had to let go and work on issues that *were* mine to own. The most honorable thing to do was to trust God to be the Rescuer, to be brave enough to turn every part of this over to Him and let the next chapters of my story unfold.

I separated from my husband and waited another entire year to see what God would do. I stopped intervening. I stopped trying to suggest the next thing I hoped would help. I stopped making sug-gestions to God. And I stopped feeling helpless. I allowed natural consequences to happen.

I thought it would be the most terrifying year of my life. But I came to realize, it was actually less terrifying to remove my hands from the situation, accept reality, and let God do what only He can do. The greatest source of my suffering was my refusal to accept what I could not change.

Toward the end of that year, there had been glimpses of a possible turnaround, but then things got dramatically worse not better. My friend Laci called it "the bitter end." The last part of a long journey when I would have to fight not to let all the bitterness that came at me, stick to me. Enough had been stolen from me.

A few weeks before I filed for divorce, I received a gift that absolutely stunned me.

A girl named Julie, who I went to college with and hadn't seen in thirty years, found my childhood Bible in a box of old books she'd stored away after graduation. She knew some of my family members worked at a local restaurant and since we now lived in the same town, she dropped off my Bible with the kindest note. Eventually, the Bible made it to my daughter who then brought it to me. She said, "Mom, the spine of the Bible is broken so when you open it, it just falls open to this one place where you had a verse highlighted from all those years ago. And you're not going to believe what the verse is."

It was Ephesians 5:3–7:

> But among you there must not be even a hint of sexual immo-
> rality, or of any kind of impurity, or of greed, because these are
> improper for God's holy people. Nor should there be obscenity,
> foolish talk or coarse joking, which are out of place, but rather
> thanksgiving. For of this you can be sure: No immoral, impure
> or greedy person—such a person is an idolater—has any inher-
> itance in the kingdom of Christ and of God. Let no one deceive
> you with empty words, for because of such things God's wrath
> comes on those who are disobedient. Therefore do not be part-
> ners with them.

Near the verse I had written some notes in my teenaged girl handwriting that very much applied to what I'd been wrestling through with the divorce. We both looked at each other with con-fidence in knowing this was confirmation of the hardest decision I've ever made in my entire life.

Later, when I told my counselor this story and showed him the

Bible, he was as awestruck as I was. He said, "I often have my clients write stories as adults speaking to their younger selves. I've never had a time where a child wrote something that arrived decades later as the perfect instruction to themselves as an adult."

It's not that I needed this to give me the courage to take the next steps I knew it was time to take. It's that God cared enough to make sure I felt His comfort as I walked out the final steps of this very long and deeply sad journey.

Again, it was poignant. But this time it was not a stabbing pain but more like a tender reminder that redemption can still be my story even if it doesn't look the way I thought it would.

A week after I got my Bible back, I was in another long session with Jim when I was processing this story and sharing how hard it was to see the divorce papers. He has been with me and my family through almost every part of this tragedy that turned everything upside down over and over and left none of us unscathed. So many times, I've said to Jim, "I don't know how much more I can take." He would always reply, "Lysa, every woman has a breaking point. There's a point of no return. When you get to the end, you'll know."

It took me years.

I think I'll be processing the good and the unhealthy reality of this experience for years to come. But there did come a moment when I knew. I literally felt something break inside of me. I wanted to talk it through with Jim because I was worried that this breaking would reduce my ability to fully love and trust others in my life—my kids, my friends, the people I do ministry with. Did that breaking now mean that I'm broken?

Without hesitation Jim said, "Lysa, I don't think that was the moment you broke. I believe that was the moment you healed."

Dang. I needed that.

What hurts

us will not be

our full story.

— ujs

Later that night, I walked through the doorway of my house knowing, with more assurance than ever, I would make it.

I went to my closet and pulled open the drawer where I keep my jewelry. I took out my wedding ring. I held it in my hand, closed my eyes, and finally knew what to do with it. I tucked my wedding ring inside my childhood Bible. It was as if these two objects were bookends of my life. A little girl who dreamed of a life that would be hers and the grown-up woman I've now become. Two different seasons carried inside of my heart, woven together with the common thread of trusting a God who loves me endlessly (even with my imperfections) and pursues me daily.

The greatest joy in life isn't when it all works out like we hoped it would. It's when we experience the God of the universe pausing to reach us and remind us we aren't alone. What hurts us will not be our full story. And this broken world isn't our final destination. With God, there's so much more.

The secret is not to get lost in the heartbreak, stuck in all that seems so unfair, or paralyzed by our own mistakes along the way. I closed my eyes and let a few more tears fall. Again, I whispered, "Good bye, good bye, God be with you, good bye." And I put the Bible and the ring in a box high on a shelf in my closet next to some pictures and cards marking both the poignant and the precious realities of life.

Wisdom to Turn to When Our Boundaries Are Called into Question

When you've been in a tough relationship for a long time, you can feel like you've lost home base. Like the safe place you return to after a long day of running hard is no longer there. You aren't sure if you are running from someone or running to someone because the relationship feels like a confusing mix of both.

You've had a clear vision of this person's potential. You love them. And there are parts of you that feel it would be impossible to let go of what's good about them. And maybe this time will be different—I mean, what if you give up right when it's about to finally get great?

What you've waited for, hoped for, prayed for, and worked so hard for seems as if it's just ahead. If you draw a boundary and make a change now, you might miss the epic moment when their potential lines up with reality.

But then you know that's not true. Remember? Home base isn't there. You know it because the next time you get hurt, and there's always a next time, you won't know where to run. Toward them? Away from them? Around and around in circles of dysfunction you go.

And the worst part of it all is that you feel guilty for wanting to make changes. Actually, you feel awful. And it's not just because of what they've said to you. All the most hurtful statements are what you say to yourself because you're a woman who wants desperately to do the right thing. And you know the right things are informed by biblical truth. So, you have a sense that it's just not right to make changes in a relationship if those changes are going to cause the other person any kind of hardship at all. It's easier to manage the hurt inflicted on us rather than the hurt we could potentially cause someone else if we set a boundary.

So, you keep trying. You keep carrying weight you aren't designed to carry. You keep paying the consequences of someone else's choices. You keep saying yes. You keep giving in, just praying you don't give out. Maybe one more time of extra grace from you. Maybe one more time rescuing them. Maybe one more time looking the other way and suddenly they will turn a corner and bring home base back to you.

You know this isn't the way that it works. But you want to believe that maybe this time it will. Maybe you'll be the hero. Maybe they will be the exception. Maybe they'll change.

You hold up statements you believe to be true and preach them to yourself like a rallying cry. And then you drench your pillow once again because you know you can't keep doing this.

I'm not sure why I just wrote all of that as if it's you. When it's me. Sometimes these thoughts are in my mind because of what other people have told me or accused me of when I've tried to set boundaries to get to a healthier place. Here are some statements running through my head:

- *The more I do for people, the more Christian I am.*
- *It's a sign of spiritual maturity to put others' needs before my own.*
- *If I know about a need, it's my moral duty to meet that need.*
- *If someone hurts me, wrongs me, or takes advantage of me, instead of addressing it head-on, I should just manage my feelings and see it as an opportunity to be more like Christ.*

There are good intentions in every single one of those statements above. And on the surface, many of those mindsets have a noble sense of self-sacrifice and Christian character. They even hint so closely at some well-known Bible verses that they seem like the right way to react. Surely, this is exactly what Jesus modeled when He laid down His life for others, right?! So, we hold up our WWJD bracelets without checking these human assumptions against the true meaning of Scripture meant to save us, free us, and teach us how to have healthy relationships with others.

I polled some of my friends on social media to see which verses they had been beating themselves up over in relation to boundaries and goodbyes, or ones that others had weaponized against them when trying to set clear guidelines for a relationship. Let's look at how we may have misinterpreted a few of these verses, what they really mean, and how we can respond if we find ourselves in a conversation with someone who calls our boundaries into question by using Scripture inappropriately.

But I tell you, do not resist an evil person. If anyone slaps
you on the right cheek, turn to them the other cheek also.

Here's how this verse has been misinterpreted:
A good Christian always overlooks being wronged and when
mistreated, she lets it go and doesn't address it.

Here's what this verse actually means:
This verse speaks to an important principle of what to do when
someone wrongs you. Jesus does not intend for us to test the limits
of the example but for us to embrace the principle of the example.
This means we are unwilling to respond to an offense with an
offense but rather display maturity.

This could be as simple as walking away from a heated conversation without attacking or retaliating against the other person.
By keeping calm, we remain in control even when the other person
is acting out of control. When we do this, we are demonstrating
that the other person doesn't have the power to make us trade our
dignity for a cheap comeback.

In the ancient world, getting slapped in the face was an offense
aimed at the dignity of a person. What Jesus intends in Matthew
5:39 is to remind us, when our dignity is violated, not to validate the
abuse by doing the very same thing to the other person that they did
to us. They already hurt us. But they hurt us double when we allow
their wrong behavior to turn us into someone we are not. This verse
is in no way perpetuating or welcoming abusive behavior from others.
It's simply saying that if someone does something hurtful to us, we
won't react in ways that intentionally hurt them right back. In this
way, we are declaring with our response that abuse is not acceptable
and therefore will not be tolerated or demonstrated by us.

If someone uses this verse against you when you need to communicate a boundary, here's how you could kindly and confidently respond:

I'm very thankful you are bringing up this Scripture verse. It's crucial we use the Truth of God to help guide us and direct us, especially when we're not seeing eye to eye on something. Here's what that verse is actually teaching us: Don't retaliate or attack when someone offends us or wrongs us. Jesus doesn't want us to sink to the level of returning evil for evil. I'm so thankful that Jesus never teaches that abuse of any kind should be tolerated or perpetuated. I'm drawing a boundary so I can stay safe and keep my heart from getting so wounded in our situation that I lash out in return. Since my heart is motivated by love and health, that's what I want to be evident in my actions.

PHILIPPIANS 2:3-4

Do nothing out of selfish ambition or vain conceit. Rather, in humility value others above yourselves, not looking to your own interests but each of you to the interests of the others.

Here's how this verse has been misinterpreted:

It's selfish to have and express your own personal needs. Looking out for the interests of others without caring about your own interests is what demonstrates humility and pleases God.

Here's what this verse actually means:

The key to this verse is the word *humility*. What does it mean to have a type of humility that values others? What does this not mean? It doesn't mean that we have no regard for our needs and limitations. It does mean rightly understanding that only God is limitless in His ability to give to and care for others. We, as humans, are limited. To recognize this isn't selfish. It's actually honoring the fact that there is a God, but you aren't Him. Therefore, we don't allow ourselves to get so drained emotionally, bankrupted financially, worn out physically, or frustrated relationally that we have nothing left to value and care for others.

Another word to pay attention to here is *interests*. This is cautioning us to evaluate whether we are doing something just to feed our pride, one-up other people, or make ourselves appear to be better than others. What keeps this in check is to make sure we aren't blowing off others' needs because of our own ambition or conceit. But in humility and honesty we are simply acknowledging what is and is not realistic for us.

This scripture invites us to care for and consider others' needs while also maintaining and taking responsibility for our needs. This is more of a warning to us so that we don't elevate our needs to a place that will compromise God's will for us and how He desires us to live in relationship with other Christians.

If someone uses this verse against you when you need to communicate a boundary, here's how you could kindly and confidently respond:

One of my greatest joys is to cheer on those I love and support their endeavors. And at the same time, I'm responsible to not extend myself past what my budget allows, therefore, I can't continue to give you money. In no way is this an indication that I don't care—I do. I'll just need to show my care and support in a different way.

JOHN 15:13

Greater love has no one than this: to lay down one's life for one's friends.

Here's how this verse has been misinterpreted:

The greatest act of love you could show is to lay down your own life for the good of others, even when it's to your own detriment.

Here's what this verse actually means:

Remember, Jesus literally laid down His one glorious life one time and it was for a high and holy purpose. Jesus didn't lay down His life to enable evil, perpetuate unholy or irresponsible behaviors, or to try and keep others happy.

When Jesus makes this statement, He is speaking within a context when friendship in the ancient world was truly valued and sought after. This type of "friendship involved(s) the sharing of confidences, [and] possessions."[1] Love expressed and experienced between friends is a beautiful thing and shouldn't be dismissed or overlooked. In our daily lives, we should want to share, and, within reason, give to our loved ones and friends. Here's the caution: we can be a resource for them when needed, but we should not become the source of what sustains them.

The instruction here isn't so much about our willingness to literally lose our life or sacrifice our needs to the point of self-detriment. Rather, Jesus is reminding us to have a willing spirit to show and extend a type of love that is honorable and willing to be self-sacrificial when necessary.

If someone uses this verse against you when you need to communicate a boundary, here's how you could kindly and confidently respond:

I agree that Jesus taught us to echo His spirit to be honorable and willing to be self-sacrificial when and if necessary. I am willing to be a resource for you when needed, but it's not realistic for me to become *the* source that sustains you. And it's also not realistic or biblical for me to sign on to rescue you from the consequences of choices you made that I had no say in.

My greatest desire is to be a cheerful giver like God says He loves, so I'm intentionally cautious not to perpetuate anything that doesn't line up with my definition of what's good and right. Please know, I am not judging you or criticizing you, I'm just staying true to only supporting what is right and healthy. Here's the benefit to us both: if I'm honest with you about what I can and cannot do, it will help prevent simmering resentments and that awkward tension that can quickly erode relationships. I don't want to try to control you or change you. I want to love you and stay in a healthy enough place that I can authentically be there for you as much as I can.

GALATIANS 6:2, 5

Carry each other's burdens, and in this way you will fulfill the law of Christ. . . . For each one should carry their own load.

Here's how these verses have been misinterpreted:

No matter the cost, it's biblical to step in and pick up another person's burdens. It's our Christian duty and obligation to help others carry their heavy loads when they're struggling and in need—this could be emotionally, financially, spiritually, or in other ways as well.

Here's what these verses actually mean:

We must pay close attention to two key words in these verses *burdens* and *load*. Sometimes we can think that it's our place to engage in an *exchange* of burdens with those people we are in a relationship with. In other words, we feel pressured to think it's our role and responsibility to take up and carry their burden for them.

Instead, we need to walk alongside them, sympathizing with their hurt and doing what we can to help ease the ache and hardship of the burden that's been placed on them.

But there may be a nuance to this that we are overlooking, especially since verse 5 teaches that each one should carry their own load. There's a difference between helping someone bear the weight of a burden placed on them (verse 2) and the load referenced in verse 5. Someone's load could be the burden of their everyday responsibilities or the consequences of poor choices they made.

"In Galatians 6:2 the Christian is bidden to 'bear the burdens' of others, in the sense of sympathizing with them in their troubles. Here (Galatians 6:5) he is told that he must 'bear his own load,' in the sense that he must answer directly to God for his own actions. His responsibility cannot be shifted on to others."[2]

If someone uses this verse against you when you need to communicate a boundary, here's how you could kindly and confidently respond:

I love to help, and I love you, so of course I want to help ease the stress of you feeling as if you've taken on too much this year. I acknowledge it is hard to be the chairman of the school fundraiser this year while you have so many other things on your plate. While I cannot be *the solution* and take over this role for you, I am happy to bring *some solutions* that are realistic for my schedule. Here are two things I can do to help you. _____ and _____. I just can't carry the weight of the entire fundraiser.

1 CORINTHIANS 13:5

It [love] does not dishonor others, it is not self-seeking, it is not easily angered, it keeps no record of wrongs.

Here's how this verse has been misinterpreted:

To maintain a posture of love and forgiveness, we should choose to forget the unhealthy patterns of behavior, destructive choices someone is making or has made, and hurtful or harmful interactions that have occurred with this person.

Here's what this verse actually means:

This verse has more to do with "counting up" or "holding on" to things that have been done against us. It's not telling us to blindly forget or ignore actions that we are still suffering the impact of. While we can forgive the fact of what happened, it may be crucial to still discuss and process the impact those actions had on you for the sake of healing. A good question to ask ourselves is this: Am I bringing up something from the past for the sake of hurting someone or for the sake of healing from what they did to me so we can both move forward?

We want to make sure we don't allow past issues to be brought up consistently or used against the other person cruelly. The phrase "[love] keeps no record of wrongs" in the original Greek could also be interpreted as assuming the best of people unless by doing so you start to accept or perpetuate harmful actions from them. In other words, don't live a life always assuming or expecting the worst of people, but do pay attention to reality. One New Testament scholar summarizes this by saying that we should not contemplate evil about others.[3] Instead, we should use wisdom and discernment to correctly know when we are safe to give access again to someone who has hurt us and when to exercise appropriate caution. Remember, God does tell us to forgive, but reconciliation is dependent on someone's willingness to not continue doing harm to us. Our goal shouldn't be to hold onto the pain that person caused so we can weaponize it against them later. It should be to one day share a testimony of what we've been through by focusing less on what happened and much more on the transferable wisdom we gained along the way that could help others.

If someone uses this verse against you when you need to communicate a boundary, here's how you could kindly and confidently respond:

Did you know that for every hurt done to us, there is both the fact of what happened and there is also the impact of what those actions cost us emotionally, physically, or financially? Please know, out of obedience to God, I have made the choice to forgive you for the facts of what happened. And, at the same time, I'm trying to understand the impact that all this has had on me. When I am processing what happened, I'm not keeping a record of wrongs to use against you. I'm just working through the impact of the pain to get to healing. So, these boundaries I'm establishing aren't a violation of Scripture but rather a verification that I'm doing the necessary work that proper healing requires.

1 PETER 3:1-2, 5-6

Wives, in the same way submit yourselves to your own husbands so that, if any of them do not believe the word, they may be won over without words by the behavior of their wives, when they see the purity and reverence of your lives. . . . For this is the way the holy women of the past who put their hope in God used to adorn themselves. They submitted themselves to their own husbands, like Sarah, who obeyed Abraham and called him her lord. You are her daughters if you do what is right and do not give way to fear.

Here's how this verse has been misinterpreted:

A wife should always obey her husband's wishes, desires, and direction, even if it is ultimately harmful, manipulative, demeaning, dysfunctional, controlling, or violating God's instructions on marriage. In order to maintain a biblical and godly marriage, the woman's wants and needs should come second to the man's.

Here's what this verse actually means:

Part of the process of interpreting Bible verses and then applying them involves reading verses in the larger biblical context. This is vitally important in this situation. First, we have to read about submission within the context of the new identity that we have in Christ. Paul, in Galatians 3:28, says there are no longer distinctions of identity or human separation that devalue the person. There is no Jew or Greek or male or female. Both man and woman depend mutually upon each other (1 Corinthians 11:11). This means we have to understand submission through a lens of equal human dignity. Submission that leads to undignified or degrading behavior is unacceptable. Christian counselor Leslie Vernick puts it this way: "God is not a God who loves men more than women or husbands more than wives. He is not a bully, nor does he sanction the behaviors of the oppressor over the oppressed. He cares for the weak, the downtrodden, the bullied, and the oppressed (Psalm 9:9; Psalm 34:18, Psalm 146:7)."[4]

So, when Peter asks women to "submit" to their husbands, he is recognizing an ancient cultural situation in which the wife would be required through marriage to submit to their husbands, which would have meant adopting the husband's religion. But for the Christian this is seriously problematic and impossible if her husband doesn't follow God.

These women who gave their allegiance to Jesus were in a tough spot because they couldn't submit and adopt their husbands' religion without dishonoring the one true God. So, because they couldn't embrace their husbands' religious beliefs and practices, they had to find other ways to honor God with their actions toward their husbands. It is an invitation to consider the very best ways we can honor God and be a witness to a spouse. But again, submission is not a license or an invitation to accept and endure degrading, damaging, or humiliating actions against us. Submission should never dehumanize a woman but always maintain the dignity and value placed on women by God. And submission should not elevate a man as superior to a woman but always cause him to be servant-hearted as he submits his heart daily to God.

If someone uses this verse against you when you need to communicate a boundary, here's how you could kindly and confidently respond:

I am committed to honoring what is honorable because, above all else, my heart belongs to God. So, I want His words to be the words that shed light on why this boundary is biblically accurate and personally necessary. Submission that leads to undignified or degrading behavior is unacceptable (Galatians 3:28, 1 Corinthians 11:11). Hebrews 13:4 says, "Marriage should be honored by all, and the marriage bed kept pure, for God will judge the adulterer and all the sexually immoral." It is not my place to judge you, but it is my responsibility to protect myself from being degraded, deceived, and devastated by your choices. Your actions are not in line with the purity being referenced in God's truth.

Lately, your version of truth has not been lining up with the facts. This isn't an accusation against you, and this isn't based on assumption or opinion. This is based on your actions and what actually occurred. Therefore, this boundary will need to be in place until I can verify that trusting you again is safe and that honoring the purity of our marriage bed is not just my commitment but yours as well.

ONE LAST THING TO NOTE:

These verses are just a starting point for us as we unpack the truth of what Scripture reveals for us to apply in our relationships. Please know: God never, ever promotes or tolerates abuse or mistreatment. Period. His Word is life, a lamp unto our feet, showing us the very next step to take in His abundant love, correction, and protection. Remember, God's Word will sometimes convict us. We don't want to brush off a prompting from Him to think or act differently. But something we should keep in mind: there is a difference between feeling conviction that should lead us to Jesus in repentance and condemnation that makes us feel as if we have to run *away* from Jesus in shame. God's Word should not be weaponized against us or used to bully or shame us. In fact, His Word is designed to heal us. Psalm 107:20 says, "He sent out his word and healed them and delivered them from their destruction" (ESV). If you ever feel like a verse is being used against you, take time to really dig deep into the meaning. Talk with a trusted friend who studies Scripture, process with a Christian counselor, talk to your pastor, look at commentaries where reliable Bible scholars help unpack verses and their context, and ask the Lord to reveal His intention and heart through the power of the Holy Spirit with these instructions. Finally, look at the principle of the verse and look at the Gospels to see how Jesus handled this principle in the midst of doing life with other people.

Getting the Help You Need

Dear friend,

For some of you this book will be exactly what you needed to help you handle a hard situation or relational dysfunction. But for some this book might be the starting place for your healing or for realizing you need to remove yourself from an unsafe or unsustainable relationship. Because I'm not a licensed counselor and this book doesn't take the place of therapy, please know there are some difficult realities in life that you will want a licensed Christian counselor to help you navigate. Please be honest about your need for counseling help. I am so thankful for the professionals who have lovingly helped lead me through my darkest days. It's always been important to me that the professional counselors I've seen have a deeply committed personal relationship with Jesus and understand the battle must be fought in both the physical and spiritual realms. A great resource to find a Christian counselor in your area is the American Association of Christian Counselors at aacc.net. With counselors in all fifty states, their heart is to connect people who hurt with people who help.

I'm praying for you, dear friend.

Much love,

My heart is very tender and compassionate toward anyone facing this harsh reality. I wanted to provide this information, both as a point of compassion and clarity around what abuse is and how to potentially find help if you're in an abusive situation.

In an article published by *Psychology Today*, I found this definition of abuse:

> Abuse within families is behaviorally nuanced and emotionally complex. Always, it is within a dynamic of power and control that emotional and physical abuse is perpetuated.
>
> Abuse may manifest as physical (*throwing, shoving, grabbing, blocking pathways, slapping, hitting, scratches, bruises, burns, cuts, wounds, broken bones, fractures, damage to organs, permanent injury, or even murder*), sexual (*suggestive flirtatiousness, propositioning, undesired or inappropriate holding, kissing, fondling of sexual parts, oral sex, or any kind of forceful sexual activity*), or emotional (*neglect, harassment, shaming, threatening, malicious tricks, blackmail, unfair punishments, cruel or degrading tasks, confinement, abandonment*).[1]

So, what does the Bible say about abuse, and what do we do regarding forgiveness in situations like this? Let's look once more at what Paul wrote to Timothy:

> But understand this, that in the last days there will come times of difficulty. For people will be lovers of self, lovers of money, proud, arrogant, abusive, disobedient to their parents, ungrateful, unholy, heartless, unappeasable, slanderous, without self-control, brutal, not loving good, treacherous, reckless, swollen with conceit, lovers of pleasure rather than lovers of God,

having the appearance of godliness, but denying its power. Avoid such people. (2 Timothy 3:1–5 ESV)

I'm thankful for verses like these that clearly state to avoid abusive people. But exactly how this is carried out is so very complex. It's impossible to put a broad, sweeping formula on top of hard relationships. There are so many factors that must be sorted out with people trained to recognize danger and to help lead those in abusive situations to know what to do and how to do it.

Here are some things to consider:

- It is good to have wise people speaking into our lives and to process life concerns with godly mentors and trusted friends. Here's a good verse to help discern people of wisdom in your life:

  > Who is wise and understanding among you? By his good conduct let him show his works in the meekness of wisdom. But if you have bitter jealousy and selfish ambition in your hearts, do not boast and be false to the truth. This is not the wisdom that comes down from above, but is earthly, unspiritual, demonic. For where jealousy and selfish ambition exist, there will be disorder and every vile practice. But the wisdom from above is first pure, then peaceable, gentle, open to reason, full of mercy and good fruits, impartial and sincere. And a harvest of righteousness is sown in peace by those who make peace. (James 3:13–18 ESV)

- These trusted friends and godly mentors speaking wisdom into our lives can help us recognize behaviors that cross the line and should be brought to the attention of a professional counselor educated on the issues at hand or, in more urgent situations, to the attention of authorities.

If you need to find a professional Christian counselor in your area, both Focus on the Family and the American Association of Christian Counselors have recommendations listed on their websites, or your church may also have a list of trusted Christian counselors they recommend.

Please know, friend, you are loved, you are not alone, and you don't have to walk through this without help. Remember, the person who is hurting you needs help that only trained professionals can give them. Getting the proper authorities involved isn't being unloving . . . it's actually for your safety and theirs.

Acknowledgments

There are so many people whose fingerprints could be found throughout these pages. It would take me another entire book to properly thank everyone . . . the people who have walked beside me, prayed for me, processed this message with me, and even lent their own experiences that made their way into the writing of this book. I am forever grateful for you, your friendship, and for the honor of doing life with you.

To the team who worked alongside me day in and day out on this book, more than helping me get the words right, you helped me get the living of this message right.

I had resistance, you offered assurance.

I had doubts, you offered confidence.

I had so many uncertainties, you offered head nods and enthusiasm that this was the book to write next.

I had dangling participles and wonky verb tenses, you offered editorial wisdom.

I had misspellings and mixed metaphors, you offered smiling emojis with your corrections.

I had theological and therapeutic questions, you offered well-researched answers.

I had unorganized files, you offered the beauty of the Google doc.

I had lulls where I got lost in all my overthinking, you offered conversations and brainstorms and your very best thoughts.

I love you. I love working together, processing life together, being honest about our struggles while studying together, and celebrating our victories together. And I really love that we found our way to this message and worked through this message . . . together.

Hope, Michael, Taylor

Meredith, Leah, Shae, Joel, Amanda, Madi, Kaley, Meghan

Tori, Alison, Kelsie, Micaela, Anna, Haley, Victoria, Melanie, Morgan, Claire

Barb, Glynnis, Lisa

Jim Cress

Janet, Janene, Mark, Tim, Erica, Don, MacKenzie, John, Meg, Emily

Candace, Mel, Lisa W.

And a special thank you to my Early Reader Group who read the earliest version of this manuscript and helped me turn it into a book worth reading.

Notes

Chapter 2: Naming the Tension That We've All Been Wrestling With

1. Ludwig Koehler et al., *The Hebrew and Aramaic Lexicon of the Old Testament* (Leiden: E.J. Brill, 1994–2000), 649.
2. B. Pick, "Precepts, the Six Hundred and Thirteen," *Cyclopædia of Biblical, Theological, and Ecclesiastical Literature* (New York: Harper & Brothers, 1894), 494. For clarity, the 613 laws include requirements that have in mind both blessing and consequence. This is such an important reminder that God's establishment of boundaries is not purely punitive but also includes instruction for the kind of life God wants us to live.
3. "What Is Iniquity? Its Meaning and Importance in the Bible," Christianity.com, March 13, 2019, https://www.christianity.com/wiki/sin /what-is-iniquity-meaning-and-importance-in-the-bible.html.

Chapter 3: It's Not About the Problems, It's About What the Problems Represent

1. Luis Villareal, "Counseling Hispanics," in *Healing for the City: Counseling in the Urban Setting* (Eugene, OR: Wipf and Stock Publishers, 2002), 220.
2. Derek Kidner, *Proverbs: An Introduction and Commentary*, Tyndale Old Testament Commentaries 17 (Downers Grove, IL: InterVarsity Press, 1964), 118.

3. "Proverbs 17:18, REV Bible Commentary," REV Bible, accessed May 19, 2022, https://www.revisedenglishversion.com/Proverbs/chapter17/18.

Chapter 4: God Takes Boundary Violations Very Seriously and So Should We

1. G. K. Beale, *The Temple and the Church's Mission: A Biblical Theology of the Dwelling Place of God*, ed. D. A. Carson, New Studies in Biblical Theology 17 (Downers Grove, IL: InterVarsity Press, 2004), 69.

Chapter 5: You Are Already Doing This Really Well

1. *Trauma*: both the act and the effect of a deeply distressing or disturbing experience.
2. Christopher Wanjek, "Stress Causes Headaches, Scientists Confirm," Live Science, February 19, 2014, https://www.livescience.com/43507-stress -causes-headaches.html.
3. Gary L. Thomas, *When to Walk Away: Finding Freedom from Toxic People* (Grand Rapids, MI: Zondervan, 2019), 13.

Chapter 6: They May Never See Your Boundaries as a Good Thing

1. APA Dictionary of Psychology, s.v. "emotional maturity," American Psychological Association, accessed May 19, 2022, https://dictionary.apa .org/emotional-maturity.
2. APA Dictionary of Psychology, s.v. "emotional immaturity," American Psychological Association, accessed May 19, 2022, https://dictionary.apa .org/emotional-immaturity.
3. John H. Elliott, *1 Peter: A New Translation with Introduction and Commentary*, Anchor Bible vol. 37B (New Haven: Yale University Press, 2008), 853.
4. Elliott, *1 Peter*, 853.
5. Rick Brannan, ed., *Lexham Research Lexicon of the Greek New Testament*, Lexham Research Lexicons (Bellingham, WA: Lexham Press, 2020).
6. Franco Montanari, *The Brill Dictionary of Ancient Greek*, ed. Madeleine Goh and Chad Schroeder (Leiden: Brill, 2015).

Chapter 7: Just Because They Say It Doesn't Mean You Have to Own It

1. Lysa TerKeurst, *Uninvited: Living Loved When You Feel Less Than, Left Out, and Lonely* (Nashville: Thomas Nelson, 2016), 259.

Chapter 8: Trying to Make Someone Else Happy Shouldn't Be Your Definition of Healthy

1. David W. Pao, *Colossians and Philemon*, Zondervan Exegetical Commentary on the New Testament: (Grand Rapids, MI: Zondervan, 2012), 173.

2. Interestingly, Colossians 3:5 gives us more clothes of defeat like sexual immorality, which could also bring some truth to why the wife above wasn't at all off base addressing pornography.

Chapter 9: What Am I So Afraid Of?

1. Origen, "De Principiis," in *Fathers of the Third Century: Tertullian, Part Fourth; Minucius Felix; Commodian; Origen, Parts First and Second*, ed. Alexander Roberts, James Donaldson, and A. Cleveland Coxe, trans. Frederick Crombie, The Ante-Nicene Fathers 4 (Buffalo, NY: Christian Literature Company, 1885), 313–14.

Chapter 10: Can a Goodbye Ever Really Be Good?

1. "The Holy Reason We Say 'Goodbye' And What to Say Instead," Dictionary.com, September 9, 2020, http://dictionary.com/e/why-do-we -say-goodbye/.

2. Wayne Jackson, "The Separation of Paul and Barnabas," *Christian Courier*, accessed May 19, 2022, https://www.christiancourier.com/articles /813-the-separation-of-paul-and-barnabas.

3. Gary L. Thomas, *When to Walk Away: Finding Freedom from Toxic People* (Grand Rapids, MI: Zondervan, 2019), 20–21.

Chapter 11: I'm Not Walking Away, I'm Accepting Reality

1. Lysa TerKeurst, *Forgiving What You Can't Forget: Discover How to Move On, Make Peace with Painful Memories, and Create a Life That's Beautiful Again* (Nashville: Thomas Nelson, 2020).

2. Leslie Vernick, "Topic: Is This an Emotionally Destructive Relationship?," Leslie Vernick: Relationship Truth Unfiltered, June 13, 2011, https:// leslievernick.com/topic-is-this-an-emotionally-destructive-relationship/.

3. Leslie Vernick, "How Do I Heal and What Do I Do About My Marriage?," Leslie Vernick: Relationship Truth Unfiltered, July 21, 2021, https:// leslievernick.com/how-do-i-heal-and-what-do-i-do-about-my-marriage/.

4. C. H. Spurgeon, *Feathers for Arrows* (London: Passmore & Alabaster, 1870), 124–25.

5. Original citation from Irenaeus of Lyons, "Irenæus Against Heresies," in *The Apostolic Fathers with Justin Martyr and Irenaeus*, ed. Alexander Roberts, James Donaldson, and A. Cleveland Coxe, *The Ante-Nicene Fathers*, vol. 1 (Buffalo, NY: Christian Literature Company, 1885), 490. We are following the Latin translation from Julie Canlis, *Calvin's Ladder: A Spiritual Theology of Ascent and Ascension* (Grand Rapids, MI: Eerdmans, 2010), 250.

6. Peter Scazzero, *Emotionally Healthy Spirituality: It's Impossible to Be Spiritually Mature While Remaining Emotionally Immature* (Grand Rapids, MI: Zondervan, 2017), 26.

Conclusion

1. Word Guru, email newsletter, wordguru.co.

Wisdom to Turn to When Our Boundaries Are Called into Question

1. Colin G. Kruse*, John: An Introduction and Commentary*, 2nd ed. Eckhard J. Schnabel, Tyndale New Testament Commentaries 4 (London: InterVarsity Press, 2017), 371.

2. *Ellicott's Commentary for English Readers*, s.v. "Galatians 6:5," Bible Hub, accessed May 19, 2022, https://biblehub.com/galatians/6-5.htm.

3. Roy E. Ciampa and Brian S. Rosner, *The First Letter to the Corinthians*, Pillar New Testament Commentary (Grand Rapids, MI: William B. Eerdmans Publishing, 2010), 647.

4. Leslie Vernick, "How Do I Heal and What Do I Do About My Marriage?," Leslie Vernick: Relationship Truth Unfiltered, July 21, 2021, https://leslievernick.com/how-do-i-heal-and-what-do-i-do-about-my-marriage/.

Some Important Notes to Consider on Abuse

1. Blake Griffin Edwards, "Secret Dynamics of Emotional, Sexual, and Physical Abuse," *Psychology Today*, February 23, 2019, https://www.psychologytoday.com/us/blog/progress-notes/201902/secret-dynamics-emotional-sexual-and-physical-abuse.

About the Author

Photograph by Meshali Mitchell

Lysa TerKeurst is president of Proverbs 31 Ministries and the author of more than twenty-five books, including *It's Not Supposed to Be This Way* and the #1 *New York Times* bestsellers *Forgiving What You Can't Forget* and *Uninvited*. But to those who know her best she's just a simple girl with a well-worn Bible who proclaims hope in the midst of good times and heartbreaking realities.

Lysa lives with her family in Charlotte, North Carolina. Connect with her on a daily basis, see what she's working on next, and follow her speaking schedule:

Website: www.LysaTerKeurst.com
(Click on "events" to inquire about having
Lysa speak at your event.)

Facebook: www.Facebook.com/OfficialLysa
Instagram: @LysaTerKeurst
Twitter: @LysaTerKeurst

If you enjoyed *Good Boundaries and Goodbyes,* equip yourself with additional resources at:

www.GoodBoundariesAndGoodbyes.com
www.Proverbs31.org

Proverbs 31
MINISTRIES

About Proverbs 31 Ministries

Lysa TerKeurst is the president of Proverbs 31 Ministries, located in Charlotte, North Carolina.

If you were inspired by *Good Boundaries and Goodbyes* and desire to deepen your own personal relationship with Jesus Christ, we have just what you're looking for.

Proverbs 31 Ministries exists to be a trusted friend who will take you by the hand and walk by your side, leading you one step closer to the heart of God through:

Free *First 5* Bible study app
Free online daily devotions
Online Bible studies
Podcasts (You might find Lysa's Therapy and Theology
 series very helpful as you continue your pursuit of
 staying spiritually and emotionally healthy.)
COMPEL Writers Training
She Speaks Conference
Books and resources

Our desire is to help you to know the Truth and live the Truth. Because when you do, it changes everything.

For more information about Proverbs 31 Ministries, visit www.Proverbs31.org.

An Invitation from Lysa

Photo by Meshali Mitchell

When my family and I were trying to heal from the darkest season of our lives, I kept praying that we'd one day be able to use our experiences to help others find healing. But I didn't just want to do this at conferences. I've dreamed of inviting friends like you over to my home to break bread and share our broken hearts, face-to-face, heart-to-heart. So I'd love to invite you to Haven Place—a safe space for you to find the biblical and emotional healing you've been looking for.

If you'd like more information on the intimate gatherings, Bible studies, and retreats we'll be having here, please visit lysaterkeurst.com/invitation-from-lysa.

I truly believe healing, hope, and forgiveness will be the anthem songs, prayers, and shouts of victory that will rise from this Haven Place.

A HEALTHY WAY TO HAVE HARD CONVERSATIONS

by Lysa TerKeurst and Jim Cress

Relationships don't usually die because of conversations that were had but rather ones that were needed but never had. So how do we talk about hard things in a safe and loving way?

Whether the purpose of the conversation you need to have is about establishing good boundaries or figuring out how to say goodbye, Lysa and Jim have created 12 practical guidelines that will help provide a healthier environment for challenging discussions.

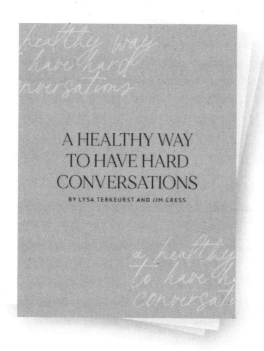

Download this resource for FREE today at
proverbs31.org/boundaries

Companion Bible Study
also available

Study Guide plus Streaming Video
9780310140351

Available wherever books are sold.

What should I read next?

These two books from Lysa go hand-in-hand with what you're learning in *Good Boundaries and Goodbyes*

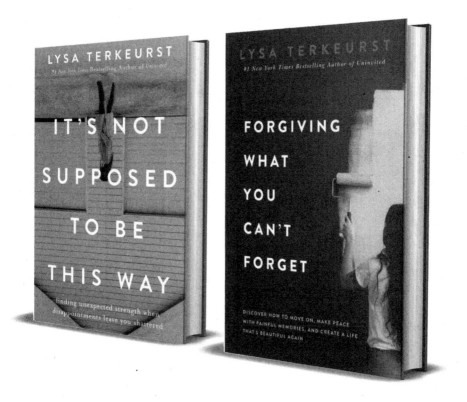

Available wherever books and ebooks are sold